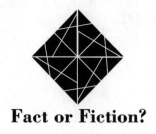

Fact or Fiction?

Astrology

Other Titles in the Fact or Fiction Series:

Fact or Fiction?

Astrology

Kelly Wand, Book Editor

GREENHAVEN PRESS

An imprint of Thomson Gale, a part of The Thomson Corporation

Detroit • New York • San Francisco • New Haven, Conn. • Waterville, Maine • London

Christine Nasso, *Publisher*
Elizabeth Des Chenes, *Managing Editor*

© 2007 Thomson Gale, a part of The Thomson Corporation.

Thomson and Star logo are trademarks and Gale and Greenhaven Press are registered trademarks used herein under license.

For more information, contact:
Greenhaven Press
27500 Drake Rd.
Farmington Hills, MI 48331-3535
Or you can visit our Internet site at http://www.gale.com

LIBRARY OF CONGRESS CATALOGING-IN-PUBLICATION DATA

Astrology / Kelly Wand, book editor.
   p. cm. -- (Fact or fiction)
  Includes bibliographical references and index.
  ISBN-13: 978-0-7377-3506-2 (hardcover : alk. paper)
  ISBN-10: 0-7377-3506-6 (hardcover : alk. paper)
  1. Astrology. I. Wand, Kelly.
  BF1708.1.A86 2006
  133.5--dc22

                                   2006027871

Printed in the United States of America
10 9 8 7 6 5 4 3 2 1

Contents

Foreword

> *"There are more things in heaven and earth, Horatio, than are dreamt of in your philosophy."*
>
> —William Shakespeare,
> Hamlet

> *"Extraordinary claims require extraordinary evidence."*
>
> —Carl Sagan,
> The Demon-Haunted World

Almost every one of us has experienced something that we thought seemed mysterious and unexplainable. For example, have you ever known that someone was going to call you just before the phone rang? Or perhaps you have had a dream about something that later came true. Some people think these occurrences are signs of the paranormal. Others explain them as merely coincidence.

As the examples above show, mysteries of the paranormal ("beyond the normal") are common. For example, most towns have at least one place where inhabitants believe ghosts live. People report seeing strange lights in the sky that they believe are the spaceships of visitors from other planets. And scientists have been working for decades to discover the truth about sightings of mysterious creatures like Bigfoot and the Loch Ness monster.

There are also mysteries of magic and miracles. The two often share a connection. Many forms of magical belief are tied to religious belief. For example, many of the rituals and beliefs of the voodoo religion are viewed by outsiders as magical practices. These include such things as the alleged Haitian voodoo practice of turning people into zombies (the walking dead).

There are mysteries of history—events and places that have been recorded in history but that we still have questions about today. For example, was the great King Arthur a real king or merely a legend? How, exactly, were the pyramids built? Historians continue to seek the answers to these questions.

Then, of course, there are mysteries of science. One such mystery is how humanity began. Although most scientists agree that it was through the long, slow process of evolution, not all scientists agree that indisputable proof has been found.

Subjects like these are fascinating, in part because we do not know the whole truth about them. They are mysteries. And they are controversial—people hold very strong and opposing views about them.

How we go about sifting through information on such topics is the subject of every book in the Greenhaven Press series Fact or Fiction? Each anthology includes articles that present the main ideas favoring and challenging a given topic. The editor collects such material from a variety of sources, including scientific research, eyewitness accounts, and government reports. In addition, a final chapter gives readers tools to analyze the articles they read. With these tools, readers can sift through the information presented in the articles by applying the methods of hypothetical reasoning. Examining these topics in this way adds a unique aspect to the Fact or Fiction? series. Hypothetical reasoning can be applied to any topic to allow a reader to become more analytical about the material he or she encounters. While such reasoning may not solve the mystery of who is right or who is wrong, it can help the reader separate valid from invalid evidence relating to all topics and can be especially helpful in analyzing material where people disagree.

Introduction

> *"In astrology the rules happen to be about stars and planets, but they could be about ducks and drakes for all the difference it would make. It's just a way of thinking about a problem which lets the shape of that problem begin to emerge. The more rules, the tinier the rules; the more arbitrary they are, the better. It's like throwing a handful of fine graphite dust on a piece of paper to see where the hidden indentations are. It lets you see the words that were on the paper above it that's now been taken away. The graphite's not important. It's just the means of revealing the indentations. So, you see, astrology's nothing to do with astronomy. It's just to do with people thinking about people."*
>
> —*Douglas Adams*, Mostly Harmless[1]

Astrology is a broad term referring to the belief that correlations exist between the apparent positions of visible celestial objects and earthly human affairs. Although not even professional astrologers agree on the extent or exact nature of these supposed correlations, the important question is whether any such relationship is possible.

Some of its defenders strongly argue that astrology has already been corroborated by modern statistical evidence. Others just as vehemently insist that only mystic forces are involved, ones which scientists are too literal-minded, biased, or obtuse to grasp, let alone measure. There are those convinced that the stars can actually predict human events on a grand scale, and others who claim they decide or guide individual human destinies. Finally, others maintain that the star positions on a person's birth date, known as their "star sign," merely indicate the likelihood that that person will develop certain personality traits.

Skeptics claim that such a wild divergence of opinions is an indication of astrology's inherently disorganized, and by extension unscientific, nature. Astrology's defenders retort that passionate debate is the cornerstone of any true science.

Can heavenly bodies influence human events? Science has independently verified that we feel the pervasive influence of cosmic influences every second of our lives. Certainly the gravity exerted by the sun and moon affects the tides, people's weight, and menstrual and mating cycles. But what about seemingly arbitrary human events predicted with uncanny accuracy, all in open defiance of the laws of chance?

Imagine that one particular morning you retrieve your newspaper and for the first time in years happen to idly glance at your horoscope, with interest born purely of ironic amusement. In just such a spirit you read, "Today your finances will experience an unexpected upsurge." You do not even bother to see whether something similar is written below any of the other signs; the entire incident is completely forgotten within minutes.

Later that day, however, a bank error in your favor arrives in the mail, making you several thousand dollars richer. Several other minor incidents occur in the space of a few hours that could to varying degrees easily be construed as financial "upsurges."

To those who believe in astrology, such an outcome was certain. The positions of the stars in the sky were recorded and interpreted by a hardworking newspaper astrologer and then written in plain English for you to read, as the stars had in fact ordained that you would.

To skeptics, however, as well as even to astrologers who consider newspaper horoscopes a bowdlerized perversion of their craft, the bank error was a sheer coincidence. In their view, the stars could not possibly have been involved, certainly not in a predictive sense let alone with such uncanny precision. Did every person on Earth born under your star sign, they would ask, happen to experience such a dramatic upswing on the same day? If they did not, does this prove your own experience was a coincidence?

If astrology lacks any scientific basis, why do so many people continue to believe in it? Even ranked alongside other paranormal fields of interest like ape-men, UFOs, and ghosts, astrology remains a lucrative global phenomenon with an enormous, impassioned following, and it has been so since the days of the earliest human civilizations. Even the most hardened cynics know their own zodiac sign, and even they will often claim that their horoscope sign "fits" their personality perfectly. But while proponents of astrology view this as yet more statistical evidence in their favor, skeptics argue that most people learn their zodiac sign early on in life and tend to assume its characteristics well into adulthood, subconsciously or otherwise, because they see it as harmless fun.

What Is a Horoscope?

By far the most influential form of astrology across the world is horoscopic astrology, which originated in Hellenistic Egypt some time between 200 and 100 B.C. Ancient Hellenistic astrology involved computing the degree of the sun's angle above the eastern horizon at a given moment, such as a person's time of birth. The astrologers call this number the "ascendant," for which the Greek term was *horoskopos*, and over the centuries the term has become synonymous with the astrological chart as a whole.

A major factor in horoscope calculation is the zodiac, the astrological name for the visible band of sky and its composition of planets and constellations over the course of an entire year, seen as a circular clock composed of twelve segments of thirty degrees each. The tropical zodiac, the type on which most Western astrologers base their calculations, begins the day of the March equinox (Aries, zero degrees) and continues clockwise all the way through Pisces exactly one year later. Although all twelve zodiac signs share names with certain constellations, for those who employ the tropical zodiac the signs themselves remain "fixed" to the days and seasons.

Another branch of Hindu origins known as the Jyotish system, however, uses the more intricate sidereal zodiac, which in addition to the process above involves painstakingly calculating zodiac signs in relation to their matching constellations. Jyotish astrologers claim that such precision is required to compensate for the parallax caused by astronomical "precession," the 25,800-year-long cycle in which the stars as seen from Earth gradually shift position in the sky. Many skeptics view this sizable discrepancy, seemingly uncorrected for in Western astrology, as a lapse in logic large enough to discredit astrology as a whole. They also note that the discoveries of Pluto and other outermost planets of our solar system ought to have severely thrown off centuries of astrological calculations, a mistake astrologers have yet to admit. The skeptics claim that astrologers, using their art all along, should have been able to predict the existence of such planets.

Astrologers like Linda Goodman retort that such factors are irrelevant because the stars themselves "remember the influence of the constellations that corresponded to them two thousand years ago."[2]

Astrology and Astronomy

Although astrology and astronomy share common origins and were at one time considered much the same thing (the study of "the heavens" in general), the two terms have vastly different meanings today. While astronomy means the scientific study of celestial objects themselves such as the sun, the planets of the solar system, comets, etc., astrology refers specifically to the alleged influence of such objects on terrestrial and human affairs. To many astrologers, their area of study involves a great deal of scientific calculations and instruments, the same ones that astronomers use. Other practitioners regard astrology more as a symbolic language, a type of cosmic divination, or an art form.

Skeptics, on the other hand, see it only as a pseudoscience. Some within the scientific community, such as Dutch-American astronomer Bart J. Bok, have published detailed essays criticizing astrology and declaiming its widespread appeal as a potentially dangerous social trend perpetrated by ignorance and primitive tribal superstition.

It is true that many ancient cultures ardently believed in astrology, a fact skeptics cite as evidence that it has little modern application. Believers, on the other hand, claim that astronomy owes its very existence to the pioneer work of ancient astrologers and note that ancient Greek astrologers were able to successfully calculate the relative positions of the sun, moon, and nearby planets with an accuracy remarkable for their time. It was not until the late seventeenth century, with the rise of the scientific method in Western society, that astronomy and astrology gradually began to mean different things: Astronomy was seen as predicting cosmic events, while astrology interpreted them.

Astronomers now regarded as geniuses, such as Galileo, Kepler, and Copernicus, also served as astrologers, although evidence suggests they did so only to help pay the bills: It was a custom of the time for the powerful and wealthy to employ personal astrologers as medieval "life coaches," as well as easier for astronomers to persuade their rich patrons to invest in building observatories specifically to improve their business-related forecasts. Many astrologers claim that Sir Isaac Newton professed a belief in astrology, yet his published writings mention the subject only briefly.

By the beginning of the nineteenth century, astrology's reputation had deteriorated from the empirical to the dubious to something that smacked of the occult.

The Mars Effect

Few credible scientists, astrologers charge, have conducted rigorous, objective research on astrology. Such a claim, in fact, was even uttered by a scientist himself, a French psychologist and statistician named Michel Gauquelin.

Before he committed suicide in 1991, Gauquelin spent the last four decades of his life attempting to determine whether astrology had any legitimacy. By all accounts, Gauquelin had been fascinated by astrology as far back as his childhood, claiming to have calculated birth charts for schoolmates by age ten (earning him the nickname "Nostradamus"). Gauquelin was passionate about discovering whether astrology could be statistically proved by compiling and analyzing large groups of birth charts. That his initial experiments, such as comparing the birth charts of twenty murderers to twenty non-murderers, proved resoundingly inconclusive by his own reckoning speaks well of Gauquelin's credibility. In 1970, however, Gauquelin wrote, "It is now quite certain that the signs in the sky which presided over our births have no power whatever to decide our fates, to affect our hereditary characteristics, or to play any part, however humble, in . . . the fabric of our lives."[3]

But by 1991, Gauquelin had come to believe in "an increasingly solid statistical link between the time of birth of great men and their occupational success. . . . What a challenge to the rational mind!"[4]

Gauquelin's most famous and controversial experiment was a 1955 study on what he termed the "Mars Effect." He claimed to have found evidence linking the rising and setting of the planet Mars (as seen from Earth) with the birth dates of prominent athletes of various disciplines, as well as physicians and generals.

Gauquelin's results were widely publicized and led to many years of heated controversy and reinterpretation. His 1956 request that the prestigious Belgian "Para Committee" of scientists conduct an independent inquiry of his findings was rebuffed continuously for eleven straight years, after which their own (reluctantly published) study using 535 European athletes as a control group appeared to corroborate Gauquelin's results. Skeptics contended for years that Gauquelin had been biased when choosing his subjects, selecting only athletes from large cities for his study. Years of further tests with groups of various sizes conducted by other groups were inevitably followed by accusations and counteraccusations of bias that reverberate to this day.

Common Arguments For and Against Astrology

Gauquelin's work notwithstanding, the consensus among most members of the contemporary scientific community is that there is no solid evidence to support astrology. They point to the lack of a single unifying mechanism astrologers agree on that could possibly enable (or motivate) stars to affect human affairs. The amount of gravity exerted by every visible planet and star combined, they say, would simply be too negligible to affect anyone born within the walls of a modern hospital.

Some astrologers rebut that causal relationships between astronomical objects and earthly events is not involved. Instead, people like astrophysicist Victor Mansfield suggest the answers may lie in emerging new fields of study still in their infancy like theoretical quantum physics, a branch of physics scientists use to study (and theorize about) universal natural processes at the subatomic level.

Still other believers speculate that astrology is a function of what the Swiss psychologist Carl Jung called "synchronicity," which referred to definable patterns or connections that cannot be rationally explained by direct causality. Instead, such patterns are the result of human behavior given the weight of reality by the "collective unconscious," a deeply buried part of the human mind that processes archetypal cultural symbols such as zodiac signs.

Skeptics claim these theories only reinforce their position that astrology is simply an example of the mind playing tricks on itself. In their view, astrology can work only in defiance of modern scientific logic (why do twins, the cynics ask, not share identical personality characteristics?), or it does not work at all. Most studies, including those published in reputable scientific journals like *Nature* and *Scientific American*, have repeatedly failed to demonstrate astrology's effectiveness in predicting people's occupations or personalities in controlled groups of any significant size. Believers, meanwhile, merely counter that such tests are biased. Most people, they argue, are not known for appraising their personalities on questionnaires with perfect honesty.

Ongoing Debate

With over ten thousand current practicing astrologers and millions of followers worldwide, astrology has never enjoyed greater popularity than it does today. A poll compiled by *Newsweek* in 1999 showed that almost 90 percent of Americans claimed to believe there was "something to astrology," while a 2002 *Harper's* magazine poll found that 45 percent of respondents believed that astrology "probably" or "definitely" was grounded in scientific truth.

The vast majority of scientists, however, condemn astrology outright. But condemnation alone does not itself disprove astrology. Neither does anecdotal evidence of missed predictions, or a lack of an acceptable causal theory, or even inconsistencies among astrological schools of thought.

By the same token, anecdotal evidence to the contrary and popular appeal do not necessarily prove astrology works, either. The pages ahead contain articles by persuasive members of both camps, all aimed at swaying your beliefs on astrology. In the end, however, it is up to you, not the stars, to evaluate the evidence and decide for yourself what you actually believe.

Notes

1. Douglas Adams, *Mostly Harmless*, New York: Del Rey, 2000, p. 148.
2. Linda Goodman, *Linda Goodman's Star Signs*, New York: St. Martin's, 1993, p. 42.
3. Michel Gauquelin, *The Scientific Basis for Astrology*, New York: Stein and Day, 1970, p. 112.
4. Michel Gauquelin, *Neo-Astrology: A Copernican Revolution*, London: Arkana, Penguin Group, 1991, pp. 79–80.

Fact or Fiction?

|Astrology Is Real

CHAPTER 1

Scientific Studies Prove Astrology's Validity

Jackie Slevin

In the following selection Jackie Slevin argues that several scientific studies performed by respected authorities in various technical fields provide evidence that star signs affect human beings in a number of ways. Citing independent experiments performed by astronomers Percy Seymour and John H. Nelson, as well as French statistician Michel Gauquelin, Slevin contends that there is considerable evidence that astronomical forces ranging from earth's magnetic field to sunspots (areas of solar activity that move across the sun's surface and appear as dark spots when viewed through a telescope) strongly affect the personalities and destinies of humans. For example, Slevin writes that Seymour's tests suggest that the positions of the constellations help determine when a fetus is "ready" to emerge from its mother's womb as well as playing a role in determining a newborn's genetic code.

Slevin also describes Gauquelin's 1951 study of 576 French doctors, which showed that the relative positions of Mars and Saturn on most of their birth dates were strikingly similar, indicating that the doctors were born with a specific calling to medicine. Finally, Slevin describes Nelson's studies of sunspots, from which Nelson theorized that the spots possess distinct "personality" and that they affect human lives on earth. Slevin also notes that Seymour, Gauquelin, and Nelson all began as cynics but became believers (or at least found themselves undecided), based purely on the data they themselves had compiled.

Slevin is the codirector of education for the National Council for Geocosmic Research.

Jackie Slevin, "Why Astrology Works," *Realta*, February 1999. Reproduced by permission of the author.

Since prehistoric times, humankind has attempted to fathom its earthly experience. Their first gesture toward this understanding may well have been a cave dweller lifting his or her eyes toward the heavens in wonder and speculation of forthcoming events. The sky could tell stories; it held omens. It foretold weather conditions, which in turn affected travel, hunting and agriculture. Daylight and darkness were measured by the rise and fall of those two majestic objects, the Sun and the Moon. The ancients used the sky as their blueprint for action. The so-called "Wise People" were those who made a thorough study of the patterns of planets and stars, and observed how to use them as signposts. Observations were made regarding how Mother Nature mirrored events in the heavens. Shellfish activity and the rhythms of the tides coincided with phases of the moon. Seafaring peoples, lacking compasses, used the North Star and other constellations for navigation. The Egyptians repeatedly observed that the Nile flooded every time the star Sirius rose with the Sun. The clockwork that the ancients observed in the sky shaped and defined their annual calendars. Moreover, this time-honored system of celestial phenomen[a] *worked*.

But *how* did it work? What was the direct correlation between earth and sky? If astronomy was the study of planets and stars, then astrology fell under the definition given to it by transcendentalist Ralph Waldo Emerson. It was, simply, "astronomy applied to the affairs of men."

British astronomer Percy Seymour wrote a startling book entitled *Astrology, the Evidence of Science*, which states that certain predictions made from horoscopes can be explained logically and tested scientifically. He has wagered his professional standing by espousing such a theory and, as a result, endured much criticism. The science of astrology is no stranger to intolerant criticism and has been often considered a laughing matter. Rob Hand, astrologer, author and cofounder of [astrological software company] Astrolabe, claims that "the way the media deal with astrology is to put on the laugh track."[1]

Seymour's Theory

Seymour has earned master's and doctoral degrees in astrophysics and has served as senior lecturer at the Royal Observatory in Greenwich, England. He is currently principal lecturer in astronomy at the Plymouth Polytechnic Institute in southwest England and director of the planetarium there. "Of course I expected people to take objection to my theory," Seymour concedes, "but I didn't expect the reaction to be so vehement and irrational. Some of my colleagues here at the Polytechnic and at the Royal Astronomical Society simply dismiss the idea without reading the book or even looking at the evidence. Meanwhile, many other scientists, even respected scientists, have evoked the cosmos—the theories that are a little short of bizarre—to explain the extinction of the dinosaurs, or what have you. That's all right. But propose a theory about astrology and people assume you're mad.[2]

Seymour himself looked askance at astrology until 1984 when a BBC [British Broadcasting Corp.] crew interviewed him briefly on his opinion of astrology. His reply, which was standard on the question, was that he "knew of evidence to support certain aspects of it, but that I personally could not think of any mechanism to explain how the planets, the sun, and the moon might affect human life."[3] He then began to seriously rethink his pat answer to this perpetual question and discovered the mechanism that could serve as the missing link between the cosmos and humans. His theory of astrology now is plain and simple: ". . . astrology is not mystical or magical but magnetic. It can be explained by the tumultuous activity of the sun, churned to a lather by the motions of the planets, borne earthward on the solar wind, and perceived by us via the earth's magnetic field while we grow inside our mother's wombs."[4]

Gauquelin's "Planetary Heredity"

The initial evidence of [the] validity of astrology that Seymour embraced was the work of Michel Gauquelin, a French psychologist/statistician, whose rigorous method of testing astrology was to show that the placement of the planets in the horoscope is more conclusive overall than the actual Sun sign. In other words, the components are more important than the sum of their parts. In 1951, armed with the birth data of 576 French doctors who were selected to the Academie de Médecine, Gauquelin made significant progress in his research. "Having (painfully) worked out by hand the position of the planets at the hour of birth of each doctor, I made a statistical compilation of my findings. Suddenly, I was presented with an extraordinary fact. My doctors were not born under the same skies as the common run of humanity. They had chosen to come into the world much more often during roughly the two hours following the rise and culmination of two planets, Mars and Saturn. Moreover, they tended to 'avoid' being born following the rise and culmination of the planet Jupiter. After such a long and fruitless search, here I was, confronted with not one but three astonishing results—all from observing the daily movement of the planets."[5]

Gauquelin tested this new method further by subjecting to the same scrutiny the charts of 508 doctors who had not yet been elected to the Academie de Médecine. "I calculated the positions of Mars and Saturn. Once again, my doctors 'chose' the rise and culmination of these planets for coming into the world. Once again, they 'avoided' being born when Jupiter was moving through this sector of the sky."[6] The sector Gauquelin is specifically referring to is the quadrant of the horoscope which extends from the 10th house through the 12th.

Gauquelin's discovery led to more research on yet another theory of "planetary heredity," a point which bears resemblance to Seymour's theory that astrology is ". . . perceived by us via the earth's magnetic field while we grow inside our mother's wombs." Sixteen years and over 30,000 charts later, Gauquelin published his results in the book *L'Hérédité Planétaire*: "Children have a tendency to be born when a planet has just risen or culminated, if that same planet was in the same regions of the sky at the birth of their parents. Certainly, it is not a very pronounced tendency; yet bearing in mind the great number of births examined, the probability that chance should have produced so many planetary similarities from one generation to the next falls at less than a million to one."[7]

Thus, Gauquelin refuted [astronomor Johannes] Kepler who, in 1598, tried to convince others of his own theory of astral heredity: "Behold the kinships of births. You have a conjunction of Sun-Mercury; so has your son; you both have Mercury behind the Sun. You have a trine from Saturn to the Moon, he has almost a Moon-Saturn sextile. Your Venus and his are in Opposition. . . ."[8] Kepler could only put forth simplistic propositions because he lacked access to the thousands of birth times that Gauquelin was able to procure.

In discovering his mechanism to explain how the planets, the Sun, and the Moon might affect human life, Seymour claims that Gauquelin's results on planetary heredity "are the most important of all of his findings, as far as my theory is concerned. This is because they are based on objectively measurable quantities, like planetary positions and birth times, as opposed to personality traits. They also indicate quite clearly that a physical agency is involved. . . . I knew that Gauquelin found the effects he saw to be exaggerated on days with lots of magnetic disturbance, and that seemed very important to me, so I got cracking on it."[9]

The Evidence of Magnetism

Magnetic disturbances are the key to providing the ancient axiom "as above, so below," for disturbance creates perceptible action, which, in turn, can be observed and analyzed. After all, Seymour's theory of how astrology works is based on magnetism. The way a womb might perceive magnetic stimulus is through the nervous system. In the same way that a baby resembles his parents in terms of physical characteristics, so its magnetic antenna is similarly wired, and resonates to the mother and/or father's same magnetic frequencies. Seymour reminds us that the very earth itself is a magnet, surrounded by a magnetic field that is 20 to 30 times larger than the actual planet. Therefore, magnetic attractions, or "disturbances," are keenly absorbed. When a baby is ready to be born, it is a magnetic signal from a planet, received by the nervous antenna in the mother's womb, that triggers the actual moment of birth. "Astrology . . . has put the cart before the horse by crediting the planets with the power to predict personality. For Seymour feels certain it is the genes that set the personality on course and the genes that determine which planetary signal will herald the individual's birth. Astrology merely labels what nature has already ordained, but the effects that astrology describes are not trivial by any means, nor are they limited to the first moments of life."[10]

What is curious about Seymour's theory of magnetism is that, although he fully acknowledges sunspots, solar prominences, solar flares and solar winds, he never mentions the work of the patriarch of sunspot research, John H. Nelson. An amateur astronomer since boyhood and radio operator for RCA Communications, Nelson pioneered solar research and forecasting through over 25 years of rigorous experimentation. In 1946 he was given the title "Short-wave Radio Propagation Analyst," and began a course of scientific observation, the results of which ended in unexpected controversy. "We have come to realize that the Sun is doing something to the planets, or the planets are doing something to the Sun that the presently recognized laws of science cannot explain. Though sunspots have never been completely understood, I found, through careful observation, that they are predictable. Why the predictions come true is not readily apparent. When future amateurs or scientists find a scientific explanation for what is taking place in the solar system, on the Sun and in the ionosphere of the Earth, we can take the subject out of the occult and assign it a scientific basis. I am confident this will be done someday."[11]

The Chinese have been recording sunspots since ancient times, but it was the Renaissance scientist Galileo Galilei who, after viewing them with his homemade telescope, reported them to scholars in sixteenth-century Italy. Scholars at this time were connected to the Catholic Church, whose strict dogmas did not allow for much free thinking. The Church doctrine on the Sun and planets was based on Aristotle, who stated that the Sun was perfect and free of any blemishes whatsoever. After repeatedly insisting that the Sun did show black spots on its surface periodically, Galileo incurred such fundamentalist wrath he was informed that, unless he rescinded his statement, he would be punished by torture. Following exasperation and anguish, Galileo finally retracted his statement, but is said to have muttered under his breath immediately afterwards, "but I did see them."[12]

Sunspot "Trouble"

Nelson then doggedly pursued his method of experimentation. RCA constructed a solar map on which Nelson could record sunspots, after observing then with a telescope, just as Galileo did. With this map he was able to make drawings of the sunspots and place them in their proper position on the Sun. At first, research with these maps confirmed that radio frequency requirements would vary according to the number of spots from week to week, and even in some cases day to day. It was also discovered that some types of spots had more influence than others. This information enabled Nelson to develop a system of forecasting frequency changing times on a daily basis. This added to our efficiency in the handling of messages, because less time would be lost during what are known as 'frequency transition periods.' During normal conditions, it would be about two hours earlier and, during above normal conditions it could be about two hours later. Knowing ahead of time when to change was of value in both the saving of time and the saving of power.

"Getting to understand sunspots in relation to good and bad signals was much more difficult. I mapped and analyzed sunspots for about a year before I dared to try my hand at forecasting what they were going to do to the signals. Progress was made, however, during the winter of 1947–48 when I fastened a solar map on a drawing board and recorded the position of all sunspots each day that the signals were in trouble. After a few months, this map became covered with sunspots but distinctly showed a concentration of spots in one particular area of the sun's surface. This indicated to me that spots in this area were the ones causing our troubles."[13]

What yet proved to be intriguing was that each spot had its own "personality." Some spots made trouble with radio signal qualities, whereas other spots "behaved well." Nelson could find no logical reason for this. What Nelson could pinpoint after years of research was that sunspots operate in a cycle of 11 years and correlated with such events as the Sun conjunct or opposite Jupiter, Venus, Mercury and the earth.

The Defense Rests

Years after this monumental research had been well established, Nelson decided to find out more about the mysterious subject of astrology. He attended astrological meetings in New York and, afterward, decided to keep away from it, stating that, "What I have seen in their books is that astrology is a very difficult subject and frankly, I have enough to do in my own specialty."[14] After one meeting, two astrologers approached him and asked for his birth data, saying they wanted to make predictions for him. "In my business, predicting magnetic storms, I know I can make predictions either forward or backward in time. If for instance, someone asked me to tell them what magnetic conditions were on September 4, 1918, I could analyze the planetary positions on that day and tell them what it was like with considerable confidence. I reasoned that astrologers should be able to do the same thing with their data."[15] Nelson decided on a retroactive reading, asking each astrologer to tell him what he was doing on a particular date two years prior at 12:30 PM EST [Eastern Standard Time]. Three months later, he received a report from each astrologer with a detailed analysis of the date. "They were both right, in fact, embarrassingly accurate. It is beyond my comprehension how they could have done this by simply comparing the position of the planets on the day that I was born with the position of the planets on the day that they analyzed. The astrologers themselves have no logical explanation either. This puts them in the same boat with the astronomers who cannot tell why sunspots change polarity each cycle and change latitude as the cycle changes. And I find myself in a similar situation because I have no reason for the correlation that I have seen for many years between the positions of the planets and the behavior of short-wave radio signals."[16]

It is now time for the media to take off the laugh track on the subject of astrology. "A 1988 survey from the National Science Foundation found that 38 percent believed astrology to be 'very scientific' or 'sort of scientific.' Six percent confessed to changing their plans to fit their horoscope. . . ."[17] The pioneering work of John H. Nelson and the recent theory of Percy Seymour have modern scientists poised to alter their entire perspective on the celestial mechanics of the universe. If the so-called arcane axiom "as above, so below" can be formulated into a rational, proven scientific theory, then the age-old profession of astrology will have its principles vindicated, and the global population will join in comprehending the words of thirteenth century philosopher St. Thomas Aquinas, "The celestial bodies are the cause of all that takes place in the sublunar world."

Notes

1. Patricia King, in *Newsweek*, January 15, 1990.
2. Sobel, Dava, "Dr. Zodiac," in *Omni*, December 1989, pp. 63–64.
3. Ibid., p. 64.
4. Ibid.
5. Michel Gauquelin, *Birthtimes*. Hill and Wang, New York, 1983, p. 21.
6. Ibid., p. 26.
7. Ibid., p. 43.
8. Ibid., p. 39.
9. Sobel, Dava, "Dr. Zodiac," in *Omni*, December 1989, p. 66.
10. Ibid., p. 68.
11. John H. Nelson, *The Propagation Wizard's Handbook*, 73 Inc., Peterborough, NH 1978, p. viii.
12. Ibid., p. 7.
13. Ibid., pp. 20–21.
14. Ibid., p. 84.
15. Ibid., p. 85.
16. Ibid., pp. 86–87.
17. Patricia King, in *Newsweek*, Jan 15, 1990.

Chaos Theory Provides a Framework for Astrological Predictions

Michelle Jacobs

In the following piece author Michelle Jacobs reasons that a scientific framework for the accuracy of astrological predictions can be found in chaos theory, a body of thought recognizing an apparent lack of order in systems that nevertheless obey particular laws. This lack of order, or chaos, can then be seen as a sort of controlled randomness, where very small or seemingly insignificant changes can lead to increasingly complex events. Jacobs asserts that astrological predictions may operate in such a framework, where events rarely manifest themselves exactly as foretold but oftentimes come very close, as if unlimited outcomes were allowed only within specific parameters.

Jacobs describes concepts including fractals—a term used by mathematician Benoit Mandelbrot (1924–) to describe shapes that are both self-similar and infinitely complex, such as snowflakes or clouds—and attractors, states to which systems eventually evolve over time. By using the events of a specific location on a specific date—Chicago on September 14, 1994—Jacobs explains through the concepts of chaos theory how a series of seemingly unrelated events unfolded astrologically. Jacobs postulates that what appears as randomness is really the ordered workings of the universe, a universe based on an original, determined pattern that astrology helps us see a bit more clearly.

Jacobs is a professional astrologer and received her certification from the National Council for Geocosmic Research in 1995. She is a member of the Astrological Association of Great Britain and the British Association for Vedic Astrology.

We want to think about the future—it's our nature. Unlike other creatures, humans possess an acute awareness of time and we often look to the future with a sense of expectancy. Science too is concerned with the future. In fact, all sciences rely on their power to make predictions. Astrology itself has often been called the *divine science* because it not only permits us insight into the puzzles of order and chaos and gives substance to life, but it also allows us to project a moment into the future, to see what lies ahead in time—a capacity usually reserved for the gods. However, when it comes to making astrological predictions, there seems to be a limit to the accuracy one can expect to achieve. Events seldom turn out precisely as foretold but, on the other hand, they will often come close. It's almost as if the outcome had certain parameters, within which it could manifest and then within those parameters, an unlimited set of choices—a controlled randomness. Astrological prediction suggests that there is a subtle, perhaps not so subtle, structure hiding behind the static of outward appearance.

The study of nonlinear dynamics is the study of just this sort of blend of order and chaos and how it manifests in nature. . . . 'Chaos', as this young science is called, deals with predictability in complex systems—systems such as Earth's sometimes turbulent weather patterns—and although it is still a fledgling science, it has already made remarkable headway towards solving some of Nature's most baffling puzzles. Social scientists and economists are employing the basic tenets of Chaos theory in making predictions about society and market trends and biologists are putting it to use in mapping the ebb and flow of populations. In his best-selling book on the subject, James Gleick writes, ". . . Chaos has become the shorthand name for a fast-growing movement that is reshaping the fabric of the scientific establishment."

It may be said that science deals primarily with making observations of this process we call 'the universe', and science likes to reduce processes to numbers, but those numbers often seem to have a mind of their own. A mathematical model, Chaos theory comes to science out of the use of computers in the modeling of real world systems. Computers allow us to actually view the elegant beauty inherent in mathematics—something which, before now, was exclusively the domain of mathematicians. The Mandelbrot set (so-named after its discoverer, Benoit Mandelbrot), a computer-generated visual representation of the geometry of Chaos and a beautifully eerie configuration, is a structure of such rich complexity as to be almost lifelike. Changes in one variable of the set will flutter and reverberate throughout the whole, spinning off possibilities ad infinitum. It shows us how the dynamics of nature are nonlinear—rarely does she follow a straight line—and how the relatively simple nonlinear equations used to create such images as the Mandelbrot set do mimic nature. In fact, realistic computer-generated landscapes, ("fractal forgeries", as Mandelbrot calls them), are only possible because the mathematics used to generate them imitate natural processes.

Chaos and Astrology

If Chaos theory is so important to modeling the behavior of complex systems—that is, the behavior of the natural world, then perhaps it has a similar role in the complex workings of astrology, for astrology also reveals a subtle relationship between simplicity and complexity; it too imitates life. Astrology and Chaos both provide means of plotting the unfoldment of processes in time and they each allow one to get a holistic overall view of nature. So if Chaos provides an increasingly accurate picture of how creation behaves, how might we as astrologers usefully apply this model? Does Chaos provide a workable approach to the astrological? As a metaphor for how randomness and determinism interact, Chaos would appear to be very important to astrology, but in order to see whether it meshes with the astrological design, we must first match-up the gears of this mechanism with those we use in practice everyday.

Both astrology and Chaos are the study of what physicist David Bohm calls the 'implicate order', the notion of unbroken wholeness. Implicate order is the order of the hologram, in which the whole object is enfolded in each part, and each part contains the image of the whole. Ours is a holographic reality, an undivided universe where everything influences everything else in a cosmos of the ultimate complexity. *Wholeness*, where even the minutest part plays a crucial role in shaping the total picture. There is also a current trend of thinking in ecology, the *Gaia hypothesis*, which regards the planet Earth as an undivided conscious whole and where to exist at all is to exist in connection with the planet. Astrology takes this a step further, predicating a universe that is self-aware, interconnected and purposeful—an entirely integrated system. We stand in relation to our surroundings interactively—it feeding into us and we feeding into it. And, as astrologers, we employ our charts as tools for understanding this relationship. Astrology is about making correlations between one part of our system and another, the happenings *up there* and our lives *down here*. We use the chart to trace the unfoldment of an idea, a business or a human lifetime, and all of these could be thought of as systems interacting with other systems. Chaos too is involved in the investigation of how systems interact and uses its own symbols and cartography—specifically, nonlinear equations and graphs—in order to do it. . . .

The Strange Attractor

The importance of Chaos theory is derived from its new perspective on the world as dynamic and nonlinear, yet predictable. You can look at nature piece by piece, as in the reductionist method, or you can see it as a dynamic whole, and when scientists think about such things as changing dynamic systems, they plot them out on a multidimensional graph or map in a place called *phase space*. In their book about Chaos, Briggs and Peat tell how scientists who study the complex predator-prey systems at work in nature have shown that these systems exhibit certain behavior in phase space—behavior not noticeable through reductionist techniques. For example, if we examine just the activities of the predator alone, we will see how its survival as an individual depends simply on its ability to hunt and kill its prey. We need to look at the 'whole'—in this case, the entire population of predators and prey—to perceive the effect mentioned above, (the stabilizing effect of over/under predation). Phase space dimensions attempt to *represent all the variables of a system*, and the resulting shapes on this map, shapes which are called *attractors*, show how the system changes over time. Even the most complicated systems of nature, when plotted mathematically in phase space and followed over time, stay within a certain measure but, within this measure, the orbits of the system never intersect, indicating that the system never exactly repeats itself, but neither do the orbits wander off in unpredictable ways. In other words, the system is *attracted* to an inescapable overall behavior and the resulting shape of this creative confinement is quite distinctive. It is the shape of the *Strange Attractor*. . . .

Astrology also exhibits this type of behavior, and it too has its Strange Attractors. You see, contained within the chart's overall form are the factors of the signs and planets, and each is itself an attractor of sorts. In astrology, Saturn, for example, has often been called the planet of *manifestation*, but even a term as broad as this leaves out many of the functions and qualities attributed to Saturn. Take a look in any rulership book and you'll find lists of such things as: *gravity, solitude, icebergs, and bricks*,—things and conditions which do not seem to have the least bit in common yet, for the astrologer, these are considered to be different facets of the same jewel.

Astrology says that, at some level, all of this 'Saturn fallout' is self-consistent and connected, that there is a sort of devolution on the part of the cosmos—a path of descent—in which *Saturn* makes its appearance here at our level in images, events and concrete forms. . . .

In Chaos theory, when we look at the large picture, apparently random events can be shown to happen within patterns, with the Strange Attractor representing the overall predictable state. And in astrology we can easily see the birth chart as a Strange Attractor: It outlines the pattern of the life and personality, but within that pattern there are infinite variations on the theme. Truly, each sign or planetary principle is in itself a strange attractor. Each contains a full potential of self-similar or fractal expressions, but these expressions never fall outside the attractor. An astrological planet contains all of its possible presentations within the overall predictable form of the planetary symbol.

Time also has its fractal dimensions, and whenever we switch one increment of time for another—as we are in the habit of doing in astrology—we are making practical use of these self-similar fractal-time dimensions. Progressions and directions are not only symbolic, as some astrologers have called them, they are also *fractal expressions of the whole* and, in regarding the astrological chart as fractal, we begin to see that there are many systems within the system, many wheels within wheels. What are harmonics if not the *fractalization* of the birthchart?

If the phenomenon called the *Strange Attractor* in modern non-linear scientific observations describes a tendency for any dynamic system to produce recognizable patterns where only random chance was formerly considered the most reasonable, exactly what does this say about astrology? Why do people and situations tend to develop astrologically characteristic patterns of identity if all of life's influences are purely random? Why, with all the choices before me, am I attracted to being like the patterns in my birth chart? The answer must be that, at some level, all this apparent randomization is attracted to a central point which, at the most comprehensive and generalized level, is predictable.

Consider the polymorphism of astrological symbols, or how in the astrological chart the same dynamics apply to any context. We use the same symbols to describe an infinite number of personalities, situations and eventualities. Astrological influences can only really be described as possibilities, and it is very difficult to anticipate the movement of the events they instigate. In this respect astrology is somewhat like atmospheric physics or a weather report. The meteorologist looks at the general state of the system and then, within that, he looks for clues as to the sorts of events which might present themselves; if there are clouds in the sky, it might likely rain. The same is true of astrology—we know that certain planetary configurations present a certain *climate* and, within that climate, certain events are likely to occur, but how can astrologers claim to know what they know? How is it that we are able to track the events of a person's life and say that this or that circumstance belongs to this or that planet? Just as life on earth could not exist without a predictable general climate, the astrological chart could not function if there were not generally predictable components. The very fact that we can make predictions—or interpret the chart at all with some degree of success—implies that, at some level, these factors are predictable and reliable. Is it feasible to regard the general factors of astrology as basins of attraction or, even yet, as *Strange Attractors* whose ultimate natures are fractal? . . .

A Look at One Day

On September 14, 1994, the city of Chicago experienced a series of mishaps, all seemingly unrelated. A power outage shut down the regional air traffic control center and brought O'Hare International Airport to a virtual standstill for one and one half hours. Computer failure at the Chicago Board of Trade, the world's busiest commodities exchange, shut down all activity until noon that day. And MCI (the long distance telephone company) had their service disrupted for about two hours by a problem with a software switch. These problems began in the morning at about 8:45 am. An astrological chart drawn up for Chicago at the time the troubles began shows Mercury rising and forming a T-square with a Moon/Uranus/Neptune conjunction, in turn opposing Mars. By astrological standards this is a tightly dynamic configuration—squares, and hard aspects in general, are considered in astrology to be the enabling irritants for creation—and this T-square was being made especially potent by its angularity. We can see how Mars, being directly at midheaven, could signify breaks and severences—in opposition to the Uranus/Neptune conjunction: abnormal situations possibly involving electrical lines and computer technology—and this axis in T-square configuration to Mercury, bringing in communication, travel, commodities exchange. Cosmic commands will make themselves known whenever and wherever they can, and here we have an example of how one configuration presented itself in different yet very self-consistent ways. There was an overall direction to the configuration yet it fractalized into a number of situations.

When planets are especially active, as in the case above, things tend to manifest as bunches of odd coincidences. But because they manifest in self-similar ways, and always as one of a whole, we can trace their presence in events up to the higher, more comprehensive level. Now, when concrete predictions are attempted, it must be realized that what appears here on our level is the end-product of a fractalization process which begins at a much higher, and more inclusive, level. There is a hierarchy of manifestation, from above to below, with the macrocosm generating the process. Each planet is a bundle of meaning—an attractor—which manifests at the lower levels in concrete forms and situations. And this is the challenge, for at the event level we encounter the vast multiplicity where manifestation relies on available conditions and contingency. We can say that the chart configurations represent the climate, but what form the precipitation will take, where it will fall and to what degree—rain, hailstorm, or full-blown hurricane—we often cannot tell. The event, the final entity emerging out of the general climate, is a special instance and more or less a product of what appears at our level as local randomness.

In Chaos theory, a structure of global determinism and local apparent randomness creates a stable arrangement that is self-similar at many scales: fracticality. Fractals are both order and chaos—they produce a configuration which is at one level predictable, and at another level unpredictable. Astrology, like Chaos, is connected with the notion of sensitive dependence on initial conditions of the system and each has its strange attractors—the definitors of equilibrium within the system. But as the system develops, predictability breaks down—the *one above* is pushed into bifurcation, multiplicity and infinite complexity. As a system evolves over time, small changes amplify through feedback with the environment; there is an exponential progression of complexity and this imposes strict limitations on predictability. The quantity of data becomes unmanageable and the quality of the data deteriorates rapidly. We can certainly say that all happenings have astrologically appropriate moments, but not everything contained in those moments will be able to manifest at that time. Nor can we yet calculate all the permutations of a planet and its combinations for a given time period. . . .

The Chaos Behind Predictions

Why are specific predictions so difficult? The problem is not that events are random but that the factors which influence them are so numerous and sometimes so obscure that we haven't got any means of making sensible allowances for them in our equations. This is what justifies astrological method, in which, following on fractal logic specifically, we make the assumption that although we can't see all the necessary detail, it is reasonable (on the basis of historical empirical data) to assume that there will be a fractal similarity between events occurring under similar overall astrological conditions. So what appears to us as local randomness is not really that at all. It is locally 'insufficient data'. The obvious consequence arising from this is that as our data improves so will our accuracy of prediction. So even if we have to limit ourselves to very general predictions at the moment, it need not always be so. In a sense, this problem is not really a limitation of astrology, it is a limitation of our understanding of causation generally. . . .

The planets and our destiny are linked by a common cause—the planets represent the closest and largest usable cosmological fractal-fragment of the original pattern, and we can study this in detail primarily in order to perceive the patterns being woven here at the micro-level. Apparent randomness is a fractal result of the original cause, and that primal cause is deterministic. The program itself was set in motion countless eons ago, from then on it's all inevitable—just a matter of whether you know about it or not. As astrologers, if we can track each development closely enough (even if initially only in retrospect) to be able—come something like an eclipse—to recognize this is at least one of the potential catastrophe points, then the rest is a matter of being able to estimate the presence or absence of significant small-scale structures and their probable manifestation within the attractor for the moment in question. But is absolute certainty impossible? The M-set appears to be infinite, and the event level seems to include facts which, on the scale at which astrology operates, is incredible in its detail, but the Universal level does not appear to include randomness—disorder. It's all organized and completely deterministic. Perhaps it's only our own inability to see this order within the fractalization of events that makes it appear to us as random. Unpredictability? No—trickier geometry, that's all.

Astrology Conforms to Scientific Laws

Percy Seymour

In the view of skeptics, astrology is based purely on fanciful speculation and faith rather than on scientific principles that can be studied and measured under laboratory conditions. In the following selection Percy Seymour argues that science itself is based on speculation and the willingness to test theories rather than the blind adherence to established ideas. Astrology, Seymour claims, is simply one attempt among many to understand the workings of the universe based on the evidence at hand: stars and humans. The scientists who claim to have refuted the validity of astrology through experiments and statistical analysis have used flawed methods and made fallacious arguments, Seymour writes. In contrast, the truly great scientists, such as physicist Richard Feynman, argue that it is crucial to science for its practitioners to remain open to ideas some too easily dismiss as "flimsy speculation." In Seymour's view, astrology is a science that, like all sciences, still contains many unanswered questions that require further research and explanation.

Seymour is a professional astronomer and researcher. His books include The Scientific Proof of Astrology *and* The Third Level of Reality: A Unified Theory of the Paranormal.

D ebate and controversy is essential to scientific progress. This has always been the case. At every age in history there have been rival theories concerning a great variety of natural phenomena. Furthermore, very often the orthodox or establishment view has not been the view that remained in favor in the light of new evidence collected by later generations.

There are some scientists who believe that we have found "scientific truth," that is, that we have discovered the most im-

Percy Seymour, *The Scientific Basis of Astrology*. New York: St. Martin's Press, 1992. Reproduced with permission of Palgrave Macmillan.

portant principles that govern the physical world. Such people feel that human scientific endeavor has brought us to a full understanding of the universe, and all that needs to be done now is to refine, clarify, and harmonize the various models which we already have. It does not require much reflection to see that this is a limited and dangerous point of view. It is also patently wrong, as any unbiased examination of the present state of scientific knowledge will demonstrate. But human nature craves the apparent security of certainty, and in much the same way as religious leaders can defend dogma against the opposition, so modern science has "sects" who wish to see "scientific truth" as absolute and superior to the pagan view of the "infidels" who believe that this is not the case.

Certainty in Science

Two professional astronomers, R. B. Culver and P. A. Ianna, wrote a book called *The Gemini Syndrome*, in which they roundly condemn astrology. In this book they quote [American psychologist] Abraham Maslow's statement: "Science is the only way we have of shoving truth down the reluctant throat. Only science can overcome characterological differences in seeing and believing. Only science can progress." The authors themselves add: "The evidence—objective descriptions of nature—is the only basis of truth."[1]

The aim of these men may be a genuine wish to be objective, and to cut through muddled and half-baked thinking which can cloud judgment and deny progress. Such a laudable aim, however, is unfortunately neither simple nor easy to achieve. However much science and scientists claim to be objective, and to seek objective "truth," the task is just as difficult for them as it is for any of us.

People who are convinced that objective "truth" is available through science would do well to consider modern developments in physics and the philosophy of science, and to con-

41

template the history of scientific ideas. Let us look at some opinions of those who have done this.

Dr. Jacob Bronowski, in his book *The Ascent of Man,* said with reference to twentieth-century developments in physics:

> There is no absolute knowledge. And those who claim it, whether they are scientists or dogmatists, open the door to tragedy. All information is imperfect. We have to treat it with humility. This is the human condition; and this is what quantum physics says. I mean that literally.

Karl Popper, the great modern philosopher of science, says in his book *The Logic of Scientific Discovery*:[2]

The game of science is, in principle, without end. He who decides one day that scientific statements do not call for any further test, and that they can be regarded as finally verified, retires from the game.

One of the most powerful and eloquent statements made in recent years on the nature of science was [American physicist] Richard Feynman's public address on "The Value of Science," which he delivered to the National Academy of Sciences in 1955. Here he said,

> When a scientist doesn't know the answer to a problem, he is ignorant. When he has a hunch as to what the result is, he is uncertain. And when he is pretty darn sure of what the result is going to be, he is still in some doubt. Scientific knowledge is a body of statements of varying degrees of certainty—some most unsure, some nearly sure, but none absolutely certain.

He continued in the same vein:

> Now, we scientists are used to this, and we take it for granted that it is perfectly consistent to be unsure, that it is possible to live and not to know. But I don't know whether everyone realizes this is true. Our freedom to doubt was born out of a struggle against authority in the early days of science. It

was a very deep and strong struggle: permit us to question—to doubt—to not be sure. I think that it is important that we do not forget this struggle and thus lose what we have gained. Herein lies a responsibility to society.[3]

Speculation in Science

It is not unheard of for some scientists and science writers to dismiss as "unsupported speculation," "flimsy speculation," or "sheer speculation" new ideas with which they disagree, do not understand, or which they feel might threaten those theories that they do support. These people give the general impression that speculation has no place in science, and that those who indulge in it are being unscientific. They also quite often support the skeptical tradition as if it were the only virtue in science. Yet the history of science has provided many examples where those who dismissed new speculative ideas turned out to be wrong, although it has also happened that on many occasions they were right.

Professor Thomas Gold, from Cornell University, once said:

> Whenever the established ideas are accepted uncritically, but conflicting evidence is brushed aside and not reported because it does not fit, then that particular science is in deep trouble—and it has happened quite often in the historic past. If we look over the history of science, there are very long periods when the uncritical acceptance of the established ideas was a real hindrance to the pursuit of the new. Our period is not going to be all that different in that respect, I regret to say.[4]

When Albert Einstein first proposed the general theory of relativity one British scientist called it "high finance in speculation." At first there were few observations to support the theory, but recently there have been many astronomical observations which show that Einstein's theory is the best gravitational theory we have to date. Yet, in the process of coming to accept Einstein's model, even some highly respected scientists suffered from this "hindrance to the pursuit of the new."

Enrico Fermi, the great Italian physicist, who eventually went to live and work in the United States, had a paper on a certain type of nuclear reaction turned down by the well-known scientific journal *Nature* because it involved a particle, called a neutrino, which at that stage had not yet been discovered: The journal editors thought that the ideas it contained were too speculative. The existence of this particle has been confirmed beyond reasonable doubt, and Fermi's theory is now an accepted part of nuclear physics.

On occasion the rejection of speculation can reach alarming proportions. This happened in Germany between the two world wars. Two German physicists, Philipp Lenard and Johannes Stark, both of whom had won Nobel Prizes for their experimental work, were supporters of Hitler and the Nazi regime. They were opposed to the quantum theory and to Einstein's theories of relativity. They tried to get theoretical physics outlawed in Germany, and branded this approach to physics as "Jewish speculation." They supported the view that all physics should be based on straightforward empirical deductions founded purely on experiment and observation.

On the whole, the great scientists and philosophers of science have appreciated the importance of speculation to the progress of science. Karl Popper said, "The essence of a good mathematical model is that it should embody the bold ideas, unjustified assumptions and speculations which are our only means of interpreting nature."

Richard Feynman said:

> In our field we have the right to do anything we want. It's just a guess. If you guess that everything can be encapsulated in a very small number of laws, you have the right to try. We don't have anything to fear, because if something is wrong we check it against experiment, and experiment may tell us that it's not true. So we can try anything we want.

There is no danger in making a guess. There may be a psychological danger if you bend too much work in the wrong direction, but usually it's not a matter of right or wrong.[5] . . .

Modern Objections to Astrology

The orthodox view of modern science is that astrology just cannot work. A variety of reasons are put forward to back this point of view. For example, it is pointed out that the gravitational pull of the Moon and planets cannot influence a fetus or baby, because the magnetic field of a doctor or midwife would completely swamp such an effect. Or it is pointed out that the lights in the delivery room are stronger than the radiation we receive from the planets. But let us examine what is being done here in the name of scientific criticism. A scientist sets up a simple, and usually quite naive, model: Then he shoots down the model, and from this he often concludes that no scientific theory can be constructed to explain any part of astrology.

Worse still, this naive and rather unscientific approach can often remain unquestioned and so it gets passed on from one generation of scientists to the next. I am here talking particularly about an attitude to astrology, although this attitude can and does occur more generally.

One of the most interesting aspects of my researches into the evidence for and against astrology has been to discover how unscientific scientists can be when addressing a problem outside their own particular field of expertise. Some scientists can also display contempt for the history, philosophy, and the methodology of science when constructing arguments about unfamiliar subjects, and this is particularly true in the case of astrology. The so-called scientific arguments with which many scholars clothe their objections to astrology are rather like the claims of those who could "see" the emperor's new clothes! And these people can resort to militancy and ridicule to hide the nakedness of their arguments.

There are normally three major flaws in arguments used to deny any validity at all to astrology. These flaws are:

1. Denial of the existence of any scientific evidence in favor of aspects of astrology.

2. Use of mathematical models with limited ranges of applicability to argue that astrology cannot work, but failing to point out the limitations of the models and the assumptions on which they are based.

3. Making scientific statements which are true only under certain conditions and failing to state the conditions necessary for their validity. Let us consider each of these flaws in turn.

The Rejection of Scientific Evidence

Denying the existence of evidence, or rejecting evidence because it conflicts with the currently accepted views in a particular area of science, is not a new phenomenon in the scientific community, nor did it stop with the debate on evolution. It is still with us today and not only with regard to astrology. In *Physics Today* (1990) Professor Philip Anderson, a Nobel laureate in physics, was commenting on some puzzling results in solid state physics. He pointed out the difficulties encountered by experimentalists working in this field in getting their results published. He writes: "This example appears to me to reveal a major weakness in our approach as scientists: a collective unwillingness to welcome new or anomalous results." He also said: "We don't want to lose sight of the fundamental fact that the most important experimental results are precisely those that do not have a theoretical interpretation; the least important are often those that confirm theory to many significant figures."

If this is true for an established area of science, how much more so is it true for scientific enquiries into astrology, the very mention of which can cause astonishingly emotional reactions among those who would most like to consider themselves rational and objective. . . .

Calculations Based on Naive Models

Many calculations which are supposed to disprove astrology are based on simple single-link models. These normally propose a direct connection between parts of the Solar System and the fetus. The connections usually suggested are light rays, radio waves, gravitational forces, or tidal effects (which have their ultimate origin in gravitational forces). Calculations based on these models then show they cannot account for the observed effects.

It must be stressed that these results are only true for the particular models considered and within the basic assumptions that underlie these particular models. A critic using such an oversimplified model has failed to construct a model that takes account of the complex realities of science. So, conclusions based on these calculations and then used to dismiss evidence relevant to scientific enquiries on astrology demonstrate nothing more than the lack of imagination and the ineptitude of the critic.

Using Scientific Facts That Have Limited Validity

Most scientific facts have a limited range of applicability. In fact, science progresses largely by determining whether observations based on our everyday experiences are also valid under the specialized conditions available in laboratories, where situations can be set up which are different from those of common experience. For example, the statement that water boils at one hundred degrees Celsius is a common experience for many people, but it is not valid at altitudes high above sea level, or in specially constructed vessels in which pressure can be increased or decreased.

Some of the arguments against my theory [that astrology is scientifically valid] make use of facts that have validity in a limited context, but these limitations are not stated. For example, reviewer Nigel Henbest has pointed out what he feels to be an insurmountable difficulty in my theory. He says, "A pregnant woman in a modern household will experience much stronger magnetic fluctuations from the washing machine and the food processor [than those coming from the lunar daily magnetic variation]. The regular rhythm of the storage heaters will swamp the weak lunar signal."[6]

As I already pointed out in *Astrology: The Evidence of Science*, the fields from most household equipment at more than two meters from the source is actually less than that associated with the lunar daily magnetic variation. However, his objection is most easily dealt with in the context of the theory of resonance, which is the physical and mathematical basis of my theory. According to the mathematical theory of resonance, if a system has a natural frequency *equal to* the frequency of an external force, then the system will have a large response to that force, but its response to forces vibrating at any other frequencies will be so minute it can be ignored. This is the whole basis of radio and television systems. Thus, a receiver will respond to the radio waves from the station to which it is tuned and ignore all others. This fact is utilized very frequently by most practicing scientists and engineers. The frequency of household equipment differs from that of the lunar daily magnetic variation by a factor of 2 million. By the same line of reasoning we do not have to switch off our radio sets every time we use household equipment because they also differ by a large factor. Since Henbest has an M.S. (Master of Science) in radio astronomy I would have expected him to realize this at once. This lapse in understanding can, I believe, be attributed to prejudice and an overeagerness to dismiss my theory of astrology.

Open-Mindedness

There is a basic attitude problem which underlies these fallacious arguments. We have already seen there is a reluctance to tolerate scientific speculation which, on the face of it, appears to go beyond common sense, or beyond currently accepted scientific models. Partly this arises out of an inherent conservative tendency on the part of scientists, a tendency that is approved and fostered by training, and is, up to a point, an understandable consequence of the quest for accuracy, objectivity, and all that is generally understood by a "scientific" approach. However, as has already been stated so clearly by many great thinkers, it is essential always to remain open-minded and ready to question. It is necessary to acknowledge the *possibility* of truth in new ideas, and not to act in a way that hinders looking for evidence that could increase our knowledge and understanding.

We need to consider theories in the terms in which they are expressed. The fact that a theory, formulated in mathematical terms, may lead to conclusions that offend a prevailing view, or indeed may offend our commonsense view of how things ought to be, is not a sufficient reason for rejecting that theory. Modern physics is founded on the relativity and quantum theories, and the resistance which these theories encountered initially arose largely because their conclusions offended common sense. Yet, unless enough people have been sufficiently open-minded to dare to allow for apparently untenable hypotheses, we would not enjoy today the astonishing increase in scientific and technical knowledge which result from these new ideas.

Richard Feynman said:

We are at the very beginning of time for the human race. It is not unreasonable that we grapple with problems. But there are tens of thousands of years in the future. Our responsibility is to do what we can, improve the solutions, and pass them on. It is our responsibility to leave the people of the future a free hand. In the impetuous youth of humanity, we can make grave errors that can stunt our growth for a very long time. This we will do if we say we have the answers now, so young and ignorant as we are. If we suppress all discussion, all criticism, proclaiming "This is the answer, my friends; man is saved!" we will doom humanity for a long time to the chains of authority, confined to the limits of our present imagination.

Tuning Life to the Solar System

At this point I would like briefly to restate the general form of my theory in the light of what has been said above. It is necessary to understand which areas of the theory are based on evidence which is beyond reasonable doubt; which parts are based on evidence that exists but is largely ignored; and lastly how the theory is speculation beyond the evidence.

It is now accepted by almost all scientists that the sunspot cycle affects the magnetic field of Earth, and the agency responsible for this effect, the solar wind, has been detected. It is also beyond doubt that the Moon causes tides in the upper atmosphere which give rise to electric currents, and these generate the lunar daily magnetic variation. There is also plenty of evidence that both the steady state as well as the fluctuating behavior of the geomagnetic field can be used by organisms, including man, for purposes of finding direction and keeping internal body time. This much is all well documented, and widely accepted.

There is evidence, largely ignored, that positions and movements of planets as seen from the Sun play a role in the solar cycle. Furthermore, there is some evidence—highly controversial but difficult to dismiss—that some positions of the planets as seen from Earth at time of birth are linked to personality characteristics of individuals.

This evidence exists. What my theory does is to propose an interpretation, based on this evidence, which can be scientifically tested. Very briefly the steps are:

1. Planets affect the solar cycle in specific ways.

2. The solar cycle affects the geomagnetic field.

3. The geomagnetic field affects life on Earth in certain observed ways.

4. Specifically, many species, including man, can be influenced by particular states of the geomagnetic field.

5. These particular influences appear to correlate with planetary positions.

6. I propose that the behavior of the fetus at the time of birth is linked to cycles within the geomagnetic field, which in turn are influenced by the solar cycle and positions of the planets. Resonance is the phenomenon by which the fetus is phase-locked to specific cycles. To put this in more specific terms, my theory proposes that the planets Jupiter, Saturn, Uranus, and Neptune control the direction of the convective motions within the Sun which generate the solar magnetic field. They do so because they play the major role in moving the Sun about the common center of mass of the Solar System. As the solar cycle builds up to maximum, so certain configurations of all the planets, at different stages, play a part in disrupting the magnetic field of the sun, by means of the tidal tug (due to gravitation) of the planets on the hot gases in the Sun.

Thus, the planets play a role in the modulation of Earth's magnetic field by the solar wind. I am also proposing that the tidal tug of the planets on the hot gases trapped in our magnetosphere will, because of resonance, lock some of the vibrations of the Earth's field in step with planetary movements. The resulting fluctuations of Earth's field are picked up by the nervous system of the fetus, which acts like an antenna, and these synchronize the internal biological clocks of the fetus which control the moment of birth. The tuning of the fetal magnetic antenna is carried out by the genes which it inherits, and these to some extent will determine its basic genetically inherited personality characteristics. Thus, the positions of the planets at birth are not altering what we have inherited genetically but are labeling our basic inherited personality characteristics. . . .

The Predictability Horizon

Many of our prejudices stem from the common sense theory of knowledge. We do need to realize that certainty does not come from common sense, nor does it come from science, nor from astrology. Certainty cannot come from any humanly constructed system of beliefs. Recent progress in a branch of mathematics called chaos theory has shown that even systems we thought were completely deterministic can exhibit chaotic behavior at times. This has given rise to a realization that even in macroscopic systems there is a limit to how far we can predict future behavior of such systems, on the basis of past behavior and present conditions. This limit is called the predictability horizon. In quantum mechanics we have the principle of uncertainty, and in large-scale systems we have deterministic chaos which has nothing to do with quantum uncertainty. Among other things, chaos theory suggests that there is a limit to how far we can predict motions in the Solar System and how far into the future we can predict weather.

The theory developed here, by bringing aspects of astrology into the realms of scientific explanation, seems to indicate that astrology will be beset by the same uncertainties that are now seen as an integral part of the scientific enterprise. I would say that astrology can offer us little or no hope of telling us what the future will be like, because of the complexities of the forces involved, and because of deterministic chaos within the physical systems that are likely to be involved in any theory of astrology based on the known forces of physics. But if this is the case, why bother to propose such a theory? Because we have within ourselves a desire to understand ourselves, our relationships with other people, other links with our organisms that inhabit our planet, our relationship with our local environment, and our links with the cosmos. To quote from Popper's *The Logic of Scientific Discovery*:

> I, however, believe that there is at least one philosophical
> problem in which all thinking men are interested. It is the

problem of cosmology: the problem of understanding the world—including ourselves, and our knowledge, as part of the world. All science is cosmology, I believe, and for me the interest of philosophy, no less than that of science, lies solely in the contributions which it has made to it.

I leave the final word to the great American cosmologist, Edwin Hubble:

> From our home on Earth we look out into the distances and strive to imagine the sort of world into which we are born. Today we have reached far out into space. Our immediate neighbourhood we know rather intimately. But with increasing distance knowledge fades, until at the last dim horizon we search among ghostly errors of observations for landmarks that are scarcely more substantial. The urge is older than history. It has not been satisfied and it will not be suppressed.

Notes

1. R. B. Culver, P. A. Ianna, *The Gemini Syndrome*, Pachart, Tucson, 1979.
2. K. Popper, *The Logic of Scientific Discovery*, Hutchinson, London, 1980.
3. R. P. Feynman, *What Do You Care What Other People Think?* Hymon, London, 1989.
4. T. Gold, "The Inertia of Scientific Thought," *Speculations in Science and Technology*, 12, 4, 1989.
5. R. P. Feynman, *Superstrings: Theory for Everything*, Edited by P. C. W. Davies, J. Brown, Cambridge University Press, Cambridge, 1988.
6. N. Henbest, *New Scientist*, 12 May, 1988.

Astrology Is Magic That Works

John Anthony West

In 1975 two writers named Bart J. Bok and Lawrence E. Jerome published a collection of their essays under the title Objections to Astrology. *The book was prefaced with a testimonial drafted by Bok and Jerome that was signed and endorsed by 186 leading scientists, including nineteen Nobel Prize winners. This testimonial stated that scientists in a number of fields had become concerned about the rising popularity of astrology, which they viewed more as a system of magic rather than a scientific practice.*

In the following piece John Anthony West argues that the term "magic," even when used as a pejorative, simply refers to something that works in apparent defiance of scientific law and which is not yet fully understood. West notes that the principles governing many scientific processes are also not entirely understood and that holding astrology to a higher standard is merely elitism, not to mention profoundly unscientific. Skeptical scientists, in West's view, study hypothetical phenomena like subatomic particles or quasars and do not consider them magical even though they are unable to fully explain the behavior or precise composition of these objects. West maintains that what we (and scientists) call "reality" is a matter of perception and labeling and not as objective or factual as scientists claim.

West is a writer and scholar whose other works include The Traveler's Key to Ancient Egypt *and* Serpent in the Sky: High Wisdom of Ancient Egypt.

This is the argument developed by Lawrence E. Jerome, following the essay by Bart J. Bok in *Objections to Astrology*.

Can astrology be disproved? Literally thousands of volumes have been written on the subject over the ages, attacks and

John Anthony West, "The Case for Astrology," *The Humanist*, 1975. Reprinted by permission of *The Humanist* and the author.

defenses, apologies and interpretations. Proponents have claimed astrology as a 'science' and an 'art', a true interpretation of the inner workings of the universe. Opponents have mostly attacked astrology on physical grounds, citing the old classical arguments: the question of twins, the time of birth versus the time of conception, the immense distances to the planets and stars, and so on.

But very few writers have come to the nub of the matter: astrology is false because it is a system of magic, based on the magical 'principle of correspondences' . . . (pp. 37–8)

The purpose of this article, then, is to try to provide that 'final disproof' of astrology. The plan is simple: I shall demonstrate that astrology arose as magic and that physical arguments and explanations for astrology were only attempts to associate the ancient 'art' with each important new science that came along . . . I shall prove that astrology is magic because its interpretations are based on the 'principle of correspondences', the very basic law of magic. I shall show that it was not until the Greeks—and then later in the Renaissance—that astrology began to be ascribed to physical influences of the stars, long after their magical characteristics had been established. (p. 39)

In their opening joint Statement endorsed by 186 leading scientists, Bok and Jerome were trying to have it both ways, disavowing astrology because of the distances of the planets and also because of the magical world view that is astrology's foundation. But . . . , these objections are mutually self-canceling. If there is no commanding physical reason to disavow astrology (and there is not if the correct model is employed), then the magical basis of astrology does not affect its plausibility. In other words, the magic might be wrong but astrology would still work because the physics was right, while from the magical world view proposed by Jerome 'the old classical arguments' are irrelevant and do not apply. We are pleased to find Jerome not only in full agreement with us on this point, but also pulling the rug out from under his own colleague's feet. For Bart J. Bok was among those writers guilty of erroneously attacking astrology on 'the old classical grounds ... distances of the planets and so on'. Indeed, Bok's entire argument is based upon those grounds. It is illuminating to see these two mutually contradictory views expressed within the same book by its co-authors and endorsed by 186 leading scientists.

Associations with Animal Life

Jerome then goes on to provide his own version of astrology's beginnings, drawing upon anthropologist Alexander Marshack's thesis, developed in his influential book, *The Roots of Civilization* (Weidenfeld and Nicolson, 1974). Originally raucously derided but subsequently generally accepted, Marshack's argument is that Paleolithic notations originally believed to be hunting tallies were in fact records of lunar observation (postulating an apparent scientific interest in astronomy in Paleolithic times, hence the initial antagonism. Primitive man is not supposed to have had scientific interests). Out of these lunar notations Jerome believes astrology developed, as magic supplanted early science: 'The association of lunar notations with the seasonal advent of certain plants and animals also helps explain why abstractly shaped constellations have animals' names: there was a long history of associating objects with animal life ...' (p. 41)

The constellations Gemini (Twins), Virgo (Virgin), Sagittarius (Centaur), Libra (Scales) and Aquarius (Water-Bearer) immediately spring to mind as examples of such animal-life associations. Even more convincing is their well known seasonal advent. Twins characteristically appear with the moon in June, virgins with the moon in September, balance scales proliferate in October and, as so many astrologers have observed, centaurs become a nuisance when the moon sails through Sagittarius in December, trampling lawns underfoot with their hooves and shooting arrows into the houses of innocent people.

Identical commanding logic supports Jerome's account of the development of those specific magical correspondences that, he claims, astrology is based upon. 'Thus Pisces (the Fish) is called a water sign, red Mars is associated with war, quick and elusive Mercury governs the metal quicksilver (mercury), planets in opposition are in disharmony, and so on.'

The Case for Magic

Presumably, it is the 'and so on' that explains why Aquarius, the Water-Bearer, is an air sign, why Scorpio, the Scorpion (an insect found only in the desert) is a water sign, and why Gemini, the Twins, must be an air sign, since early man would quite naturally associate twins with the air, as well as with the moon in June—how should he do otherwise?

While this reasoning is obviously good enough for 186 leading scientists, 19 of them Nobel Prize–winners, it will not satisfy nitpickers, who in this instance, may have a point. But this does not automatically invalidate Jerome's insistence that magic is the basis of astrology,

> One may well ask, Why would magic develop along with civilization? As in the case of lunar notations and seasonal time-keeping, one can only suggest that magic arose because it was of selective advantage. Perhaps magic gave the burgeoning city-state cohesiveness; one could easily make a case for magic being the power wielded by priests to keep the citizens in line, convincing them that only by working for the good of the state could they keep the 'powers of nature' in check.

> This interpretation would further suggest to a hard-core skeptic that civilization does not have a rational basis, but rather an irrational basis of *selective* value—irrational at least in terms of the twentieth century. For magic is based on the 'principle of analogies', or the 'law of correspondences', as it is generally called in astrology. As we shall see, this

'principle of correspondences' is merely a product of the human mind and has no physical basis in fact.

Later, Jerome will claim that the chief danger associated with belief in astrology is that it 'robs man of his rationality, his most human feature'. Perhaps it is not only astrology that has that effect? We find the notion that magic, that is, superstition, has 'selective advantage' especially engaging. The alert reader may well wonder, as do we, why magic should then subsequently have lost this original selective advantage? Presumably because eventually Reason accidentally arose, and Reason had even greater selective advantage? But noting that the impetus behind the Bok/Jerome book with its prestigious endorsement is precisely the Rationalists' irrational fear of a resurgence of superstition, this latter argument becomes difficult to support. The forces of Reason (Jerome) and the forces of superstition (astrologers) are both co-existing without the biological survival of either at stake. The question then imposes itself: how can two such mutually opposed forces co-exist in modern society, when both have a selective advantage? As everyone knows, a selective advantage presupposes the physical demise of the selectively disadvantaged.

The Principle of Correspondences

But it would be uncharitable to continue in this vein. It seems to us odd no one noticed that, like 'the principle of correspondences' itself, Jerome's entire argument is 'merely the product of the human mind and has no physical basis in fact'. Nor has anyone picked up on the implications of that extremely interesting latter sentence.

Astrology is indeed based upon the Principle of Correspondences; but Jerome does not understand this principle or 'the physical basis in fact' that is ostensibly his criterion. One hundred years of relativity theory and high-energy physics have made it absolutely clear that matter (the 'physical basis in fact') is itself a form of concretized energy. Every high school student knows this. Since matter is a form of energy, the question of 'reality' takes on a new, pressing and philosophical significance. How 'real' is Reality? is a question currently raised by physicists and philosophers of science everywhere. It is not easily answered within the context of modern science. But one aspect of the situation is absolutely clear and agreed upon by scientists and laymen alike: what we call Reality is largely (if not entirely) a consequence of our perception.

That is to say, we *know* that a table is comprised of atoms (whose provenance remains a total mystery, incidentally). And we know those atoms are in an eternal state of furious motion. But we perceive the solid, immobile table. The physical basis, that sacred 'fact' before which Jerome and his scientific colleagues genuflect, is demonstrably an artefact of the senses, undeniably and scientifically 'a product of the human mind' in some very profound if mysterious way. All ancient metaphysical systems understood this. It is most familiar through the Hindu concept of Maya, the illusion of the world—which, incidentally, does not mean that the world itself *is* an illusion; rather that our perception of it is illusory. No physicist would disagree with this, and a number of the most renowned physicists have explicitly written to this effect (for example, Sir Arthur Eddington famously remarked that 'the world more resembles a mind than a machine').

The Power of Perception

How then to account for our perception of the world? What is it that is responsible for our irremediably subjective notion of the physical 'facts'? It is the Principle of Correspondences.

We perceive the world as we do *only* because the atoms at their eternal dance *correspond* in a particular way with, our own perceptual faculties. In other words, if our perception were different, the physical world (and all those facts that comprise it) would be different as well. And it is the facts that would have to change accordingly. If our perception were exponentially quickened, the table would lose its solidity. We would witness a rhythmic whirr of atomic particles. If our perception were prodigiously slower, a tree would live and die within a few blinks of an eye. We would perceive it in motion (time-lapse photography furnishes a less extreme example of this) as a flickering green flame; the seasons might then appear as music, and music would be a solid.

In practice, it is very difficult to give up the conviction that the table is a fact, and has a physical basis. As all the ancient teachings insist, the grip of the senses is strong. Nevertheless, the true, energetic nature of the table is a point on which all scientists agree. Matter is but energy in infinitely varied states of harmonic equilibrium which correspond to, or resonate with our perceptive faculties in a particular way. What is responsible for that 'physical basis in fact' is the ancient Principle of Correspondences in operation. It is the Principle that is real, if anything can be said to be real. It is 'fact' that is subjective, conditional, provisional, 'illusory'.

The Magic of Potatoes

Now it is quite true that the Principle of Correspondences is the basis of magic, and of astrology. Jerome is quite right to undermine his own collaborator's credibility on this score. But he then proceeds upon the double assumption that he understands magic, and that it is invalid, neither of which are true.

Understood correctly, Magic is a name applied to the human endeavor to consciously make use of the creative powers of nature. It is the attempt to master or mimic the fundamental laws of resonance that have produced the cosmos. Whether or not such mastery or mimicry is possible on the human level does not concern us here, but the ancient understanding is certainly correct. The basis of Magic is the Principle of Correspondences. It is this principle that makes possible the transformation of energies; the mysterious phenomenon underlying all natural processes, biological, organic, and celestial.

For example, when we eat a potato, its energy is transformed, into blood, bone, muscle, tissue, and finally thought and emotion. Biologists like to call this process 'digestion' but that is just a name applied to a specific form of natural or organic magic. What is responsible for the miraculous transformation of nutrients into thought is a fabulously complex array of chemical and molecular *correspondences*. On a more fundamental level, the same principle mediated the transformation of the indigestible minerals in the soil into the organic nutrients of the potato, and on a more fundamental level still, it made possible the initial transformation of energy into its basic mineral form. Thus it is Magic that makes possible creation, indeed, all conscious, organic life. In a quite literal sense, all of perceived reality is Magic.

The ancients understood this perfectly, and in great detail. The Egyptians personified Magic and called him Heka, the primordial transforming power. It was Heka who accompanied Consciousness (Sia) at the rudder of the Solar Boat, on the fabulous journey that led from Death to Resurrection or Rebirth, since it is the transformation of the physical into the spiritual that is the only human activity of real consequence. Today, Heka is put to mundane and destructive tasks, but even so he makes science possible. Without Heka, the Principle of Correspondences, mediating between the conditional physical world and the observer, there would be and could be no science. The higher and more rarefied the energy level, the less predictable, repeatable and measurable the phenomenon, and the less exact or 'hard' the science (it is only in contemporary science that 'hardness' in this sense is a virtue; in most other human activities it is a form of stupidity. A repeatable violin virtuoso would be a laughingstock, and a predictable samurai would soon be a dead one).

Art Is Magic

Living organisms are less predictable than rocks, so biology is notoriously less 'hard' than geology, while psychology is 'softer' still—so much so that the geologic-minded are loath to call psychology a science at all. And from their point of view they are quite right. But it is Heka, Magic, the Principle of Correspondences that makes even geology possible. Meanwhile, since the study of people tends to have more immediate relevance to many of us than the study of rocks, abandoning psychology in the interests of uniform scientific hardness is not necessarily a move in the right direction. In fact, Heka has not really been disenfranchised, despite the Church of Progress. He is still very much with us. Only his role in all creative activity is no longer recognized at face value. On the cosmic and planetary level he has been deprived of consciousness, and his name has been changed to Evolution. On the human level he continues to function more-or-less sporadically as Art.

Art is magic, literally and technically. Sacred Art is objective, sacred magic, consciously based upon cosmic principles, and it works on everyone whose faculties have not been stunted or destroyed by modern education. Secular art is subjective, secular magic and it works only upon the converted: those directly affected. Bad art is bad magic, and it works only on the gullible or not at all. (Advertising, incidentally, is sorcery, which works on the will as opposed to the emotional centers.) But Art is really just a name for a specific form of magic. It is Heka, the Principle of Correspondences that allows the inspiration of Mozart or Beethoven to manifest in soundwaves (through inanimate instruments made of wood and brass) and transform itself into that exquisite rush of emotion within us. It is Heka who heals. If sick, even terminally ill patients, change their attitude towards their malady, they can sometimes be cured. The medical profession grudgingly has come round to admitting the truth of this ancient understanding, though it is not yet perhaps prepared to acknowledge the force responsible. It is Heka, Magic, the Principle of Correspondences, that effects the interchange between 'attitude' and the afflicted organs—which is an example both of 'action at a distance', and of an effect without a 'plausible physical explanation'. Try to measure 'attitude'. Astrology (when it is not debased to its pop level) operates in the upper reaches of psychology, those necessarily rarefied realms where human consciousness interacts with realms higher than our own, and to which we may aspire—if we do not restrict ourselves to the joyless scientific paradigm of Jerome and Bok, and Culver and Ianna and the world 'out there'. And inescapably, it is Heka, Magic, the Principle of Correspondences that sees to it that Divine Inspiration (Will or Intention), made manifest in the planets, transmits itself (by virtue perhaps of their chemical make-up, size, speed and orbits) in subtle frequencies and amplitudes. These in turn produce fluctuations in electromagnetic or geomagnetic fields—as yet not clearly understood or specifically identified but whose existence is acknowledged. These fluctuations are physical in a sense directly analogous to the fluctuations in the air, the soundwaves, that the ear inteprets as music, or the fluctuations in light that the eye interprets as color. In this case, those fluctuations represent celestial harmonies, and they manifest on earth as 'meaning'.

Astrology Is Valid

The study of this meaning is astrology. It was not developed by aggrandizing priests taking selective advantage of the buffaloed masses by converting lunar notations into animals such as twins, virgins, scales, centaurs and aquatic scorpions. It is the Principle of Correspondences that validates the astrological premise and that makes possible its study.

So when Lawrence E. Jerome says 'astrology is false because it is a system of magic', he is not only wrong, but very precisely wrong: astrology is *true* because it is a system of magic. And when he says, 'the "principle of correspondences" is merely a product of the human mind and has no physical basis in fact', he has actually managed to incorporate into that sentence the principal elements of the astrological situation—

something other critics have not done. But he does not understand its implications. It is 'fact' that is 'entirely the product of the human mind'. All modern physicists would agree. And fact's 'physical basis' is a consequence of the operation of the Principle of Correspondences, mediated through our own perceptual faculties. So, while Jerome is correct in saying, 'the principle of correspondences does not have a physical basis *in* fact', the statement is both meaningless and deceptive. For it is the Principle of Correspondences that is the basis *of* fact.

Having set out to provide the 'final disproof' of astrology; to show once and for all why astrology does not work, Jerome has unwittingly furnished the information necessary to show why it does; and that it must—for the Principle of Correspondences is universal. A system by definition presupposes the mutual interaction of its separate components. And the solar system is most assuredly a system. 186 leading scientists have endorsed Jerome's argument. History will accord them the respect they deserve.

Fact or Fiction?

Astrology Is Fake

CHAPTER 2

Astrology Is a Pseudoscience

Michael White

As its proponents are quick to point out, astrology is not only one of the most ancient human practices but has managed to attract a wildly popular following, including the endorsements of presidents and celebrities. Enduring popularity, however, does not make astrology a science, according to Michael White, the author of the following piece. White argues that although a few scientists have admitted the possibility that human affairs could be influenced by the positions of the stars, not one shred of evidence, statistical or astronomical, exists to back up such speculation. White observes that even the most basic astrological tenets are riddled with inherent inconsistencies. One of these is the idea that distant stars and planets exert a gravitational force that influences people's personalities and lives. He notes that according to the laws of physics, the gravitational force between a baby and her caregiver is much stronger than that between the baby and stars light-years away.

White notes that when confronted with evidence that appears to disprove astrology, its practitioners dismiss the new information as "irrelevant." Even the discovery of new planets such as Neptune and Pluto, which seem to necessitate, at the very least, painstaking revisions of existing charts and horoscopes, tends to be dismissed by astrologers, he argues.

White is the former science editor of British GQ magazine and director of scientific studies at d'Overbroeck's College in Oxford. He is also the author of many books, including biographies of Isaac Newton and Isaac Asimov.

A strology is a truly ancient practice. No one is certain when or where it began. Practitioners assign overwrought significance to its supposed origins, placing it in the ancient realm of Atlantis and suggesting that the Ancients bestowed astrological knowledge on the Sumerians and the Babylonians. The truth is probably more prosaic: the original seed of astrology was cultivated about ten thousand years ago, but where exactly remains a mystery. Some theories suggest that monuments such as Stonehenge, which are around five thousand years old, could have been constructed for astrological purposes; others place the first dabblings earlier and in the Middle East.

The oldest relic linking humans with astrology comes from a document called the Venus tablet, or the *Enuma Anu Enlil*, dated to the age of the Babylonian civilization, sometime between 1800 and 800 B.C., and containing astrological references and talk of "omens." The tablet reads: "In month eleven, fifteenth day, Venus disappeared in the west. Three days it stayed away, then on the eighteenth day it became visible in the east. Springs will open and Adad will bring his rain and Ea his floods. Messages of reconciliation will be sent from king to king."

Early Greek civilization adopted astrology, and it was placed in high esteem by the philosophers of the time. There was no delineation between astronomy and astrology from the era of the Greeks [ca. fourth century B.C.] almost until the time of Galileo [sixteenth century A.D.], and the same mathematical tools were employed to study the movement of the stars as those used to help astrologers make prophecies and personal star charts.[1]

In one form or another an abiding interest in astrology survived the Age of Reason, but it fell into decline during the late eighteenth and early nineteenth centuries, partly, it is be-

1. Galileo was, incidentally, a practicing astrologer as well as one of the first modern astronomers. However, historians believe that he "played" with astrology simply to help pay the bills and thought little of it as a "science."

lieved, because of the vogue for everything "modern"—the desperate and quite laudable clamor toward the age of technology. Isaac Newton and others had crystallized the concept of the universe as a mechanical thing—the planets held in orbit by gravity—indeed, a mysterious force, but one that could be understood using human ingenuity and mathematics. Suddenly the ancient gods and the flux of existence no longer seemed all-powerful and beyond us. As human civilization rushed headlong through the Industrial Revolution and into the era of modern medicine, modern astronomy, and a world ruled by [Charles] Darwin, [Karl] Marx, and [Albert] Einstein, belief in astrology became terribly unfashionable, an embarrassment.

Modern Astrology

Today, the art of astrology is experiencing something of a renaissance, but there is astrology and astrology, and if we are to appraise the subject properly, we must have clear definitions of what it is all about.

To the serious astrologer, newspaper gurus of the subject—the Russell Grants and Mystic Megs—are nothing more than charlatans who are merely in it for the money. To them, the nonsense we see spouted out on television shows and in the tabloid press demeans what they consider to be a serious subject based upon very strict and highly complex rules. So, effectively, for the moment, we can ignore this aspect of astrology, consign it to the intellectual garbage can; which is actually nothing more than the "serious" professional astrologer would demand of us.

However, just because high-powered astrologers who claim to be masters of a complex craft say that their work is based upon ancient and elaborate mathematical concepts does not make it true. Indeed, constructing a complete birth chart for an individual requires an element of skill unnecessary for a tabloid columnist. But actually, even this so-called technical expertise requires little more than high-school-level mathematics. To draw up a birth chart, a half-dozen factors need to be considered—fewer than a simple engineering task such as building a wall.

The astrologer needs a basic grounding in geometry and a little trigonometry, as well as a smattering of simple astronomy. But this is nothing a reasonable intelligent twelve-year-old could not manage. To coin a popular but quite apt phrase: "It's hardly nuclear physics."

As well as this quite minimal mathematical ability, the professional astrologer employs a strong element of interpretation based upon ancient handed-down wisdom. Although the "serious" astrologer surrounds his or her trade with a veneer of expertise, and frankly makes too much of the mathematical skill involved and the training required to master the art of astrology, there is also the question of motive. Expert astrologers and critics are united in condemning tabloid astrology and horoscopes, but surely the motivations and the drives of the high-brow practitioners are little different. Do they not offer fantasies wrapped up in what they like to think is complex mathematics? The only real difference between them is the market to which they appeal. In England, self-proclaimed elitist astrologers such as Shelley Von Strunckel and Sally Brompton—who is a graduate of something called the Faculty of Astrological Studies in London—write books aimed at the "highbrow" end of the popular astrology market and act as personal consultants for the rich and the famous.

Astrological Schools of Thought

Such divisions in a single practice produce an amazing range of beliefs and subsets. It is possible to see more rival disciplines within the broader sweep of astrology than any other aspect of the paranormal. So, not only do we have the upscale practitioners and the "low-brow" tabloid horoscope hacks, but there are those who believe astrology is the overriding power that shapes us, determines who we marry, what careers we take up, and our state of health. Yet others see astrology as merely a means of interpretation, a little like tarot or the use of the I Ching.

Some astrologers believe that the stars influence our health. This was an idea first popularized by the [sixteenth-century] alchemist, astrologer, and all-around mystic Paracelsus, who believed there was an intimate connection between the elements—the four substances of which, according to Aristotle, all matter was made—and the stars in the heavens. He linked the behavior of the elements, the movements of the stars, and the well-being of his patients in a triumvirate that led to an astrological alchemy that some modern astrologers still support.

Others totally disregard the advances of the past century and place far greater significance upon the influence of the stars than they do upon factors such as psychological development, genetics, or environment. An example is a book called *Life Cycles* by an American astrologer, Rose Elliot, in which it is claimed that child development has little to do with mundane factors such as nurture or nature but is controlled by astrological influence. According to Elliot, the child's behavior when they first experience "separateness" from their parents (often referred to as "the terrible twos") is not molded by anything so prosaic as the relationship between child and parent, the presence of a younger child, the personality of the child, the genetic characteristics of the child and parents, or the environment in which the child is raised. No, it is because the planet Mars returns to its birth position in the child's star chart at the age of two, and, because Mars is identified with war and aggression, it exerts a disturbing effect on the mood of the child. Obvious, really.

"System of Energies"

So, this is the background to astrology. It is a much divided subject, split into elitist and popularist groups. Like many subjects and enthusiasms, it is quite naturally composed of people with very different opinions and views and those who place different emphasis upon certain aspects of the art. It is also a very ancient practice and has its roots in the mists of history, a practice that has been manipulated and molded for different ages, but has at its heart a set of ideologies that have remained unchanged since ancient times. The astrologer believes that the planets of our solar system and the stars themselves play a fundamental role in the way we develop as individuals and what happens to us in our daily lives; that celestial objects can control our destiny and that of the world at large. To the astrologer, world events are not governed by chaos theory, a succession of random events upon which we humans try to impress our individual wishes and desires with varying degrees of success, but are instead predetermined and set in motion and maintained in equilibrium by some intangible force exerted by the planets and stars.

Let us for a moment suspend disbelief if we are skeptics, and contain our desires and wishes if we are ardent enthusiasts. How could astrology work?

Unless the influence the stars have upon our lives is due to some as-yet-unknown force, we only have conventional forces we already know about to explain it. There could possibly be other forces at work in the universe, but as science builds a clearer picture of the way the universe works, the room for new forces and strange mechanisms diminishes (although it would be extremely arrogant of any scientist to assume that all forces and all mechanisms are known). However, for the purposes of trying to work out how stars and planets could have an effect upon our lives and personalities, postulating some unknown force gets us nowhere. If we say, then, that if astrology is a true mechanism controlling the way in which we as individuals interact with the universe, we have a limited number of options.

The most popular idea has long been that some form of gravitational force is at work and responsible for the claims of astrology, that in some way the gravitational force between distant planets and ourselves causes a mysterious link so that we are all subject to this mechanism. In other words, as the stars and planets move in their paths, there is a *flux*, or force, or a "system of energies," that makes us what we are and dictates what we do. This then leads to the actions of the individual and the future of nations.

Gravity 101

The major flaw with this idea is that the force of gravity is extremely weak. In fact it is the weakest of the four types of natural forces—the weak nuclear, the strong nuclear, the electromagnetic, and gravitational force. It has been calculated that the gravitational force between a baby at the moment of birth and the midwife in the delivery room would be a million times greater than the gravitational influence of any planet in our solar system and an astronomically larger influence (literally) than the distant stars.

To see why this is so, we need only a brief consideration of Newton's discoveries about gravity made over three hundred years ago. Newton created a grand theory, the Law of Universal Gravitation, which demonstrates that every single material thing in the universe exerts a force upon any other material thing in the universe. So far, so good, for the astrologer. The problem is, not only is the force of gravity weak, it depends upon the distance between two pieces of matter and diminishes in power the further apart the objects are.

Newton showed that the way the force of gravity between pieces of matter changes over distance may be calculated using what is called an *inverse square law*. For example, imagine two planets A and B, orbiting a sun. Suppose A and B are of

Astronomist and mathematician Galileo (1564–1642) practiced astrology to make extra money. Library of Congress.

equal size, but the distance between A and the sun is half the distance between B and the sun.

This will mean that the force of gravity between A and the sun will be four times greater than between planet B and the sun. Similarly, a third planet C (of equal mass to A or B) which is three times farther from the sun than A, will experience a gravitational attraction (1/9) of that between A and the sun.

73

Everything in the universe adheres to this inverse square law. This is why the midwife (a relatively small object, but much, much closer to the newborn baby) actually exerts a far greater gravitational influence upon the child than a planet hundreds of millions of miles away.

Flawed Arguments

Often, astrologers and enthusiasts who want to believe in astrology try to use Newton's law of gravitation to produce what they like to believe are explanations for the power of planetary influence, but they miss the point completely. The most familiar argument goes something like this: "The moon creates tides on Earth because of the gravitational interaction of the two objects—the Earth and the moon—why, then, shouldn't the moon and the planets also affect the human brain? After all, we are made up almost entirely of water."

The first part of this argument is quite correct. The gravitational forces that act between the Earth and the moon, and indeed the Earth and sun, create the effect of tides. However, this is because we are dealing with very large masses. There is no comparison between the gravitational effect between the moon and such a small mass as a single human and that between the moon and the entire planet Earth.

So, what other forces could we consider as candidates to explain the claims of the enthusiasts? Well, there are actually very few. There is the *tidal force* between any two objects. This is linked to gravitational forces, but the effect of distance in calculating its influence is even greater, so this force would have even less impact upon us. . . .

The Evidence of Science

Professor Peter Roberts, author of the book *The Message of Astrology*, has suggested that the human body can somehow act as a conduit for a mysterious form of what he describes as "resonant planetary interaction." This is a pseudoscientific term conjured up to describe what Roberts believes is the influence of planets acting through some mysterious force that travels across space using a wave with a frequency sympathetic with some sort of "life force" or energy within all of us. Unfortunately he does not explain where this resonance originates, how it operates, or how it impacts on human beings, using anything other than the vaguest terms. So in effect it leads us nowhere. Roberts is joined by another scientist, an astronomer named Dr. Percy Seymour, author of a New Age tract called *Astrology: The Evidence of Science.*

The problem is, all this is again terribly vague and takes us little further than the astrologers who talk about some strange energy coming from the planets and stars. Using these muddled ideas about resonant planetary interaction, Seymour even has the temerity to try to dismiss the scientific objection to talk of external forces emanating from the cosmos influencing us at birth. In a recent newspaper article, the journalist (who was clearly on the side of astrology), said:

> Trotted out by detracting scientists time and again, the standard objection [to any form of force such as gravity influencing our lives at the moment of birth] is that the magnetic resonance of the planet is so slight that it would be swamped by the electrical equipment in the hospital, or at home by the likes of storage heaters. By way of rebuttal, Dr. Seymour proceeds as if ripping through a rather dim firstformer's test paper. "Firstly bear in mind the old trick of an opera singer shattering a wineglass. It only works when the voice resonates at the same frequency as the atoms of the glass. So, in the hospital, there's no question of planetary resonance being swamped because the electrical equipment will be operating at different—that is, the 'wrong'—frequencies. If your radio is not tuned to a sole station, you won't hear it."

These are neat analogies, but this "explanation" actually answers nothing and certainly is not an argument that rips through "a rather dim first-former's test paper." Dr. Seymour assumes that the frequencies generated by the machinery nearby would be the "wrong" frequencies, but how does he know? Where is the evidence? What single scrap of proof can he or any other enthusiast for astrology show to demonstrate irrefutably that there is a strange resonance that affects all our lives? Let alone at which frequency it operates. It is pure speculation—something I can only assume he would never allow in his official work as an astronomer.

Furthermore, what does "magnetic resonance" really mean in the sense these authors use it? Has anyone ever noticed the work of this mysterious force other than using known interactions between particles and electromagnetism, such as that at the heart of a very useful laboratory device called a *nuclear magnetic resonance spectrometer* (NMR)?

Rules of Attraction

As Professor Seymour's description shows, magnetism is one other possible contender from the armory of the enthusiast often used in an effort to define the force that is supposed to enable planetary influence. But again, magnetism is an incredibly weak property that only operates over short distances— try it yourself with a compass and a small bar magnet.

In reply to this, enthusiasts point to the fact that migratory birds are known to be able to navigate using the lines of magnetic force around the Earth. Why then, they argue, could magnetism not lie at the root of planetary influence in astrology? The answer is similar to that used to counter the astrologer's hijacking of Newton's law of gravitation. Migratory birds do not make interplanetary journeys. The lines of force they mysteriously and fascinatingly employ are powerful magnetic lines of influence that are produced by the huge iron core of *our planet*. Besides, if astrologers really want to insist that there is some sort of magnetic effect at work, then that influence would be dominated overpoweringly by the magnetic field of the Earth itself. In a sense, this is analogous to the comparison between the influence of the midwife and the planets—the impact of the magnetic field of the Earth would be vastly greater than any intangible magnetic force that has somehow reached us from the other planets of the solar system. . . .

Barnum Statements

Analysts long ago noticed that many horoscopes contained a large number of very vague statements. Examples include such waffling as: "You have considerable hidden talent that you have not yet used to your advantage," and, "While you have some personality weaknesses, you are generally able to compensate for them." Critics of astrology have dubbed such declarations "Barnum statements" after the American showman who coined the phrase, "There's a sucker born every minute."

Most strikingly, surveys have shown that when a sample of people are shown Barnum statements from horoscopes, ninety percent of them believe the statement applies to them, and can link what is said in even the most crass tabloid horoscope to events in their lives or their hopes and aspirations. The fact that on occasion these horoscopes have been either deliberately fabricated or written by hard-pressed journalists makes no difference at all. One research scientist, Geoffrey Dean, has also noted that when horoscopes contain succinct but slightly more specific personality references, such as "you have a good imagination," they are seen as less relevant to individuals reading them than the horoscopes full of Barnum statements. The reason for this is clear: with a Barnum statement, anyone can make of it what they will.

Other experiments have been, if anything, even more revealing. In a set of tests relating to his work on linking personality with properties of natal charts, Michel Gauquelin placed an advertisement in the magazine *Ici Paris* offering free horoscopes to anyone who responded to the ad. He received

150 requests and duly posted the horoscopes. He then followed this up by asking each applicant what they thought of the horoscope they had been sent. Ninety-four percent said they believed the horoscope accurately fit their personality. What Gauquelin did not tell them was that they had all received the same horoscope—that of Dr. Petroit, an infamous French mass murderer.

Star "Science"

So much for experimental and statistical analysis of what astrology claims; but what of the so-called "science" of astrology? Here, I'm afraid, this arcane study again fails to deliver.

First, we have to consider the fact that the constellations as we see them from Earth are pictures primitive humans contrived to help them understand the universe a little better. The stars that make up these constellations are not really grouped together; indeed, most are hundreds or thousands of light-years apart, and it is only from the perspective of someone here on earth that they seem to take on patterns such as the Plough or the Great Bear.

The second anomaly in the arguments put forward by astrologers is the matter of when exactly the mysterious "astrological force" is supposed to take effect. Is it not obvious that in terms of impacting on the character of the embryonic human, the moment of conception would be far more significant than the moment of birth—the point at which this new human being simply leaves one environment to join another?

But even if we ignore these problems, what is to be made of the fact that ancient astrology, which has remained ostensibly unchanged for many thousands of years, is based upon the premise that there are only six planets in our solar system? The ancients observed only Mercury, Venus, Mars, Jupiter, and Saturn. The other three planets of the solar system have all been discovered during the past 250 years—Uranus was discovered by Sir William Herschel in 1781, Neptune in 1845, and the most distant planet, Pluto, was first observed as recently as 1930.

Astronomers point out that if these three planets were unknown, then surely all natal charts drawn up before 1930 were incorrect, even if the celestial influence claimed by astrologers is real. When questioned on this, astrologers become strangely tight-lipped. If anything, their most common response is to say that the discovery of these planets makes no difference. When pushed on the matter, the popular astrologer and author of many books on the subject, [noted astrologer and author] Linda Goodman, has claimed intriguingly that "a planet does not have any astrological influence until it is discovered." A statement one would have thought undermines the entire premise upon which astrology is built.

Clearly, astrology should not call itself a genuine science. Typically, it played no role in the detection of Uranus, Neptune, and Pluto, and it has offered not a scrap of useful material toward the discovery of *anything* tangible. In fact, many practitioners of astrology are proud of the fact that the central tenets of the subject are rooted in ancient understanding. Linda Goodman has stated: "Alone among the sciences, astrology has spanned the centuries and made the journey intact. We shouldn't be surprised that it remains with us, unchanged by time—because astrology is truth—and truth is eternal."

Sadly for the enthusiast, astrology cannot be both "a science" and "unchanging"; the two are mutually exclusive. The essence of science is experiment and a willingness to question even long-established tenets of the subject. Without this, science would be a dead subject, as dead as astrology.

Horoscopes Are Meaningless

Lynne Kelly

Astrologers claim that all people born under a given zodiac sign share personality characteristics that distinguish them from people born under other signs. The diagrams astrologers create based on these signs are called horoscopes. Astrologers use these horoscopes to infer character and personality traits and to predict changes of fortune or future events based on the astrologer's interpretations.

In the following viewpoint, author and skeptic Lynne Kelly claims that the language of horoscopes is so vague that the words could mean anything. She also suggests that the ambivalent language horoscopes employ is carefully crafted to make readers believe they are receiving a personalized message. The trick to successful horoscope composition, Kelly writes, is leavening the expected optimistic commentary with quasi-negative qualifiers that sound specific and penetrating. Such is the power of words that followers of astrology consider their horoscopes a confirmation of their uniqueness in the universe. She concludes that although horoscopes do not offer valid predictions about a person's life, they are a harmless pastime.

Kelly has taught science and mathematics for over thirty years. She holds degrees in engineering and education and says that she "delights in debunking claims of the paranormal."

I sit across the table from you. Wearing coloured robes and masses of jewellery, I blend with the smell of incense to make reality seem a little less real, somehow. I have charts and images, drawings and numbers, which I consult during meaningful pauses. And this is what I tell you:

> I don't see the happy person you show to the world. I sense inner hesitancy. The world sees you as reasonably contented

but that's not what is deep inside. It is your individuality which is being suppressed, partly by your own self-doubt. You are a practical person, but there is something deep within you which wants to express itself in less pragmatic ways. You have been able to subdue it until now, but the pressure is growing for you to follow your individual path. You are not like others and find the pressure to appear so, is a dictum which is becoming more like a prison than you want to admit.

People like you, and mostly you like them. You are a friendly person who bends to accommodate others. In fact, sometimes you bend so much you nearly break. You try to do what others want of you and avoid confrontation whenever possible. Your need to do the right thing by family and friends restricts you so much. But you do the right thing almost always.

There is much inside that you keep hidden from the world. You fear the rejection which may result if you were true to your real self. There are things you would wear, places you would go and assertions you would make if only you didn't worry so much about the feelings and opinions of others. The expectations others demand of your energy constrain you so much that you worry you may never reach your full potential.

The chance is coming soon and you need to be ready for it. The planets align in such a way that travel is a key word in your path. It may be that you will travel but I feel the planets may be indicating travel in relation to an auspicious person. Someone will travel onto your stage from afar—that person will be the link to your cadence. You must be ready for that eventuality—it isn't far off now and it is essential you recognise it. Those who realise their dreams are those who grasp the opportunity when the planets are right. Your time is very soon.

Using the Reading

Ask for a date of birth and come back a day later with that date written on the top of your card with the star sign. I usually manage a 95 per cent hit rate with my one-size-fits-all astrology reading.

It's called the Barnum effect: a bit for everyone. We are far more alike than unalike. If the reading was totally positive, the client would reject it as unrealistic. It is essential that the 'negatives' also provide an excuse for behaviour and disappointments. People need to have a hope and recognise their uniqueness—none of us wants to be like most other people. As well, there is a real tendency among people to try to make descriptions fit. They will search for matches and find them.

Astrology is the most popular and widely used of the paranormal arts. It's fun and mostly it's harmless. So why not just let it be? That's for you to decide. . . .

Double Blind Testing of the Zodiac Types

When shown their reading most people can identify with some, if not all, of it. They rarely look at the readings for the other signs. Scientific method dictates a double blind testing is required. That means the person selecting the appropriate reading and the person administering the set must not know the 'expected' outcome.

The following readings have been drawn from a range of references using the traits generally accepted as typical for each star sign. Selecting which is most accurate should, according to chance alone, match the expected star sign once in every twelve. As you read each description, note how specific, yet contradictory, they sound. Ask yourself if any, in any way, fit you. Are there some aspects of your complex personality in each? Then choose the one which best suits you. We will check against the zodiac signs later.

One. Ones value freedom. Their quirky and eccentric natures make them individuals who see the next trend—they are often the ones who set it! Ones are our revolutionaries, marching to a different drum. They are our idealists and dreamers. But they are also rational, intuitive and logical. They often find it difficult to accept the limitations of a conventional society and clash with authority.

Internal conflict mixed with a conservative streak supports a conventional morality and lawfulness in their fight for social justice. Ones are often easy to identify by their unconventional dress and frenetic pace. Occupations which suit Ones include those which involve caring about others. Some love technology and are attracted to electronics or computing. The crucial aspect of any occupation for Ones is that they are challenging conventions and marching towards change.

Two. Twos are bold and confident people. They are motivated and can be very enterprising, showing leadership qualities. They like to take action, and can be headstrong and dynamic, impulsive and competitive.

Their fiery nature keeps Twos always active, rushing into new challenges but not always following through completely. Their confidence and speed lead Twos often to prefer to do things alone. Twos like careers with challenges, with the thrust of competition pushing them on. Dreaming of being racing car drivers or test pilots, they often end up in firefighting, selling, wheeling and dealing. They like things sharp, so a surgeon's job appeals. Twos like to succeed and are usually confident they will do so.

Three. Three is an emotional and sensitive sign. Threes tend to be home loving and family oriented. They like security and safety. Displaying an innate ambition they take a safer, more subtle path toward goals. Success is important but is balanced by their caring for others. They may appear to have a hard exterior, but are very soft inside. They have an unexpected tenacity and a deep and complex personality with which they hide their vulnerability. This can lead them to be very moody, their defensiveness often mistaken for shyness. Although a little prone to self-pity, they display enormous compassion for others.

They are born for the nurturing careers—social work, nursing, childcare and the service industries. Their tenacity makes them good in business, and their love of food, history and the sea often leads them to a career linked with one of these.

Four. Fours are the ambitious people—disciplined and hard working. They are determined to succeed. They are responsible people who care for society and abide by its rules. They often feel tied to obligations which may cause conflict with their determination to succeed and intrinsic ability to climb. With order dominating, especially financially, Fours are highly moral, seeking boundaries and clarity.

Childhood is often difficult due to their early maturing and then the tendency to be given, or take on, responsibilities beyond their years. Fours can be very depressed and pessimistic, but their good humour and wit helps them overcome this melancholic aspect of their personalities. Liking structure and order, they choose careers which emphasise these traits. They can achieve very high levels indeed.

Five. Fives are inquisitive and playful—eternally young. This is a sociable star sign—showing a strong desire to communicate, explore and talk. Entertaining, but easily bored, they enjoy intrigue. The duality of the sign shows that there are two sides to everything—Fives are always questioning. They gather people and ideas to feed their insatiable curiosity. They are restless and prone to nervous exhaustion, sometimes crashing into depression. They eventually spring back to repeat the cycle.

The careers which suit Fives are those based on communication such as journalist, teacher, broadcaster, writer, advertising, lawyer or salesperson. In fact, just about anything which isn't repetitious. Using their love of socialising at work, they will often achieve highly, polishing their ideas on their interaction with others.

Six. Sixes have a dramatic presence. They tend to organise everyone. Proud, enthusiastic and sharing, Sixes want to enjoy life and take everyone else along for the ride. They can sulk or become bossy if others refuse to follow. Sixes want to be special and to be loved. They are born to rule. Craving attention, they want to be singled out. Although they can become self-important at times, they are creative and generous. Their warmth is often tuned with a need to dominate, making them benevolent leaders unless opposition forces them to take a harsher line.

With a strong sense of justice, Sixes will fight for causes they believe in. Despite their strong personalities, Sixes are easily hurt but don't show their pain. Any career which allows them to control the situation and make use of their dramatic presence will suit them well.

Seven. Marriage and relationships are important to Sevens. They are in need of harmony and have a strong sense of fair play. Diplomatic, impartial and able to see both sides of an argument, decisions are often difficult for them. Sevens are often late but their charm ensures they are forgiven. They love balance in their lives, but may swing in their thinking before reaching a final stand. Avoiding confrontation, they often bend to accommodate others. Sometimes being too accommodating, they cause themselves stress. When pushed too far, Sevens demand attention, often shocking themselves and others by the unexpected outburst.

More than any other sign, Sevens need people and will adapt to maintain harmonious relationships. They tend to dress in understated good taste and choose careers which involve working with other people. They are skilled at acting in a conciliatory role while drawing on their creative and artistic natures.

Eight. Eights are described by words such as dreamy, romantic and imaginative. Their lives are controlled by the ebb and flow of their emotions. They are compassionate, impressionable and constantly concerned about the welfare of others. Eights are constantly fighting an inner struggle between emotional ties and the world's demands.

Moods rule Eights' lives. They are our artists and visionaries. Reality and illusion blend in their minds. It is their bigger picture, and their beautiful images of what life could be, which form a barrier between them and the mundane daily reality.

An Eight's compassion enables people to take advantage of their sympathy, often demanding help beyond what the Eight is able to give, and causing enormous guilt when the Eight is unable to do all that is asked of them. They are attracted to a career which enables them to express themselves in words or images—to dream about just what might be.

Nine. This is an optimistic and open-minded sign, always chasing a goal. Nines ask the big questions of life and set out to find the answers with enthusiasm. Their outgoing natures look for new adventures and new ideas. Sometimes devastatingly frank, they are always honest and tolerant, never intending to offend.

Nines value freedom of belief for themselves and others. Hating boredom, without a firm purpose they can become depressed but are usually having fun. Impulsive, innovative and intuitive, Nines often initiate but don't always follow through. They leave that to their less adventurous followers. Their vivid imaginations cause them constantly to seek new challenges and may cause a degree of dissatisfaction with life.

Nines dress casually. They enjoy sharing knowledge and continuing to learn. They love travel and sport. Due to their broad interests and constant search for new challenges, many Nines change careers mid-life.

Ten. Tens are the intense, magnetic and passionate people. They take risks without fear. Their forceful and dominant personalities rarely leave them unnoticed. Others find Tens difficult to know. They value their privacy and keep much of their personal lives hidden. Tens love power and breaking new ground.

Brooding and intense, Tens have a sharp insight. They display great empathy, preferring to understand than be understood. They can be manipulative yet compassionate, compulsive yet discerning. They resist change and their entrenched thinking can become self-destructive. They display jealousy and resentment, often bearing grudges for a long time. Tens tend to have piercing eyes and a self-contained stance. Mystery, magnetism and sexuality define a Ten. They prefer careers which use their astute minds, often creating major change within their work environment.

Eleven. Loyal, dependable, enduring, steadfast, secure and stable. That's an Eleven. Elevens find security, and a reason for being, in their partner, home and work. Their practical side often overwhelms their more artistic traits. Although cautious, Elevens are stubborn, strong and determined. They enjoy an orderly routine without insecurity or risk taking, adhering to duty and routine. This may appear to be inflexibility, but they often cope with life's ups and downs better than other signs. Elevens have a jealous and possessive nature, but can be very generous. They have a love of fine things and can be self-indulgent.

Elevens' most striking feature is their voice. They often have a beautiful singing voice and tend towards careers in the Arts. Being practical and productive, Elevens suit careers requiring stability. The world depends on its Elevens.

Twelve. Twelves are modest, restrained and refined perfectionists. They expect high standards of themselves and others. Intelligent, organised and exacting, they tend to be very practical and efficient. The conflict between a strong sexuality and morality can lead to prudishness. The desire to serve others often dominates a Twelve's life, and they become stressed by their expectations of themselves.

Attention to detail makes Twelves invaluable colleagues, but also increases the work needed to get any job done to their satisfaction. They often become workaholics. They value common sense along with hygiene, tidiness and efficiency. Well groomed, they shine in careers which draw on their organisational skills and are often satisfied with supporting roles, which they do extremely well. They display great loyalty and discretion but can become frustrated when bored.

Which one are you? Are you sure? A key to the 'correct' star signs for each of these descriptions is given at the end of [this viewpoint]. . . .

Test as many other people as you can. Have them pick you out. Have them choose the one which fits themselves and others they know well. Then check them against their date of birth. Is there any correlation with the accepted star signs? With the true signs?

Due to chance alone, you should get one person in twelve right. I have rarely done that well.

Evaluating Astrology

Most astrologers seem to genuinely believe there is a truth to what they are saying. Under test conditions, when they have been involved in the test design, many astrologers are genuinely surprised when their readings are no better than random chance predicts.

Perhaps there is something to it when we take in the complexities of the planets. Maybe we can ignore the fact that the gravitational effect of the planets is massively less than that of the table in the birth room. Gravitational pull reduces inversely with the square of the distance away. A planet is so far away it has significantly less pull than anyone near you. I rather like the fact that my husband had more gravitational influence over our daughter at birth than Mars. But then others feel differently.

The Zodiac Key

One	Aquarius
Two	Aries
Three	Cancer
Four	Capricorn
Five	Gemini
Six	Leo
Seven	Libra
Eight	Pisces
Nine	Sagittarius
Ten	Scorpio
Eleven	Taurus
Twelve	Virgo

Astrologers complain that just considering the sun sign is too simple. Many have rejected simple sun sign astrology. But if there is no correlation with the sun sign, it is a rejection of the aspect of astrology that is considered to be the core belief for most of the population.

Astrology has wonderful language and fantastic imagery. It also makes people talk about their feelings and personalities. And it's fun. Viewed from that perspective, it's harmless.

References
1. Wallaby, Sir Jim R. 1987, 'What star sign are you really?' *The Skeptic*, vol. 7, no. 3. pp. 8–9.

Astrology Relies on Unproven Claims

Ivan W. Kelly and Geoffrey Dean

Some defenders of astrology claim it is a scientific discipline and that its practitioners have made great contributions to many other fields of science. In this selection authors Ivan W. Kelly and Geoffrey Dean refute this claim and argue that astrology is not based on testable explanations, as all true science is. Instead, the authors write, astrologers rely on mythological explanations, unprovable claims, and testimonials. Kelly and Dean argue that astrology could actually become a scientific field if astrologers dropped their dogmatic attitude and tested their premises using scientific methods. However, astrologers are likely to regret this approach, the authors write, because many of their claims are likely to be disproved. Kelly and Dean further note that astrology's defenders generally fail to understand the distinction between purely theoretical notions unsupported by scientific data and ideas based on proven scientific principles.

Kelly is a psychology professor and skeptic who has written numerous articles on the topic of astrology, including "Is Astrology Relevant to Consciousness and Psi?" and "Astrology and Science: An Examination of the Evidence." Dean is a former research scientist and technical editor, as well as the author of a book-length critical study of astrology, Recent Advances in Natal Astrology.

Some astrologers and sympathetic defenders claim that scientists are often engaging in astrological research under new labels. Some examples:

> [Astrologer Valerie] Vaughan (1996a,b) says that such scientists are "intellectual land grabbers" who are "usurping en-

Ivan W. Kelly and Geoffrey Dean, "Are Scientists Undercover Astrologers?" www.astrology-and-science.com, December 8, 2000. Reproduced by permission of the authors.

tire conceptual frameworks originally developed and held by astrologers", and who are then claiming as their own their "discovery of what astrology has always known."

[German heliophysicist Theodor] Landscheidt (1989:7) says "most scientists do not realize that their findings confirm fundamental astrological ideas."

[Astrologers Geoffrey] Cornelius, [Maggie] Hyde and [Chris] Webster (1995:166) say that astrology includes "electro-magnetic fields in the solar system, the ancient metal-planet affinities, and the statistical demonstrations of the [French scientists Michel and Françoise] Gauquelins."

[Astrology software developer Michael] Erlewine (undated) says that studies on lunar activity, especially those involving geomagnetism, are consistent with astrological tradition.

[Author John Anthony] West (1991:312) says that if astrology cannot be disconfirmed then "a new branch of science may well take root", calling itself anything but astrology even though it involves "nothing but astrology."

The reasoning behind such claims is detailed best by Vaughan, so her comments will be the focus of what follows. Vaughan is the militant astrologer whose debunking of skeptics (Vaughan 1998) claimed that skeptics are ignorant, biased and misinformed. Her claim was disputed by [Ivan W.] Kelly (1999), who showed that Vaughan considers only misinformed critiques of astrology, never informed critiques, which are numerous and devastating. Her wordy, rambling rebuttal (Vaughan 2000) receives an extended reply in Kelly (2000a).

False Claims About Astrology

According to Vaughan (1996a) scientists and other academics have been usurping astrology by rewriting history and by not admitting the astrological basis of their ideas. As a result "astrological language is already being depleted and supplanted by scientific terminology: we are being dispossessed of our astrological principles."

What are these astrological principles that scientists and other academics are supposedly usurping? According to Vaughan (1996a,b) a basic astrological principle is "celestial-terrestrial correlations exist." Therefore any area is astrological if it involves things like biological clocks, bird migration, bees orientating themselves by the sun, fractal geometry, planetary patterns that correlate with anything terrestrial (weather, earthquakes, human behavior, animal behavior, the stock market). It is also astrological if it involves theoretical ideas such as the Gaia hypothesis, morphic resonance, and grand unification theories in physics. Similarly, Landscheidt (1994) includes patterns of plant growth, sunspot cycles, long-lasting weather patterns, and daily cycles in animal metabolism, under the astrology label.

Vaughan (1995) says these scientific labels are "plagiarized astrology, pure and simple, and [astrologers] should feel free to quote [such research] when discussing correct astrological prediction." Furthermore, they "are not simply new names for what astrology has known all along, they are also scientific proof that astrology works"; therefore, despite academic talk of astrology being dead, "many astrologers think we should be celebrating a revival", even though the revival is being absorbed by these revisionist "territorial grabbers" (Vaughan 1996b). . . .

Flawed Reasoning

Vaughan provides three arguments for seeing scientific research as astrology, namely history, as-above-so-below, and similarity, but none are persuasive. Her arguments are as follows:

1. History. Originally astrology consisted of natural astrology (the forecasting of natural phenomena such as tides and eclipses), and judicial astrology (the judgment and

prediction of human affairs such as wars). That is, astrology had a foot in two different camps, namely physical science and divination. So Vaughan (1996b) argues that from the earliest days "astrologers were also astronomers, meteorologists, and mathematicians", therefore astrology has original land titles to these areas. But Vaughan fails to point out that natural astrology was absorbed by science in the 17th century, so that judicial astrology is "the only meaning of astrology since end of 17th C" (OED [*Oxford English Dictionary*] 1991 edition). To argue otherwise, as Vaughan does, is like arguing that chemistry is still alchemy, or psychology is still natural philosophy, or that much of science is still philosophy and theology. But it just ain't so.

2. As-above-so-below. Vaughan says astrology involves "as above so below", so it involves anything terrestrial-celestial. But this fails because, as in (1), it tries to revive an obsolete natural astrology as modern astrology. Indeed, many astrologers flatly disagree with Vaughan, arguing that astrology deals with symbolic connections, not physical connections, so (2) [it] fundamentally misrepresents astrology's core beliefs. For example, [French electronics professor Alain] Nègre (1998) argues of physical links that "by no means should they be confused with astrology", while [author Patrice] Guinard (1997) argues that such links could never explain "the [astrological] transformations which occur at another level of reality" or support "the understanding of a birth-chart."

3. Similarity. Vaughan says that chronobiological explanations are similar to astrological explanations; for example, stellar effects on bird navigation are similar to those claimed by astrology on people (Vaughan 1996b). But they are not similar. Birds use stars in real time like street signs, which is nothing like people supposedly

acting out their lives according to stars fixed at birth. . . . To link chronobiology with astrology is not plausible.The implausibility of Vaughan's three reasons is further revealed by comparing the procedures and achievements of astrology with those of the supposedly usurping research, as follows next.

Science vs. Astrology

The scientific study of celestial-terrestrial correlations is described easily enough. It is what the relevant scientists actually do, which in broad terms is the same as in any science—they test ideas against empirical data and against competing ideas ([author Robert T.] Pennock 1999, [philosophy professor Elliott] Sober 1999). For example, the idea that birds navigate by the stars can be tested in planetariums where stellar positions and visibility can be controlled at will. Ideas that are disconfirmed are either modified or replaced by others, which are then examined and tested in turn. In other words the ultimate arbiter of success is nature herself.

Similarly, we can examine what astrologers actually do, both in their practice with clients and in their ideas given in astrology books. In broad terms, astrologers make judgments from birth charts. No chart, no astrology. But here the arbiter of success is not nature but personal experience—if it seems to work then it does work. What could be more reasonable? In fact it is quite the opposite, simply because experience can be unreliable. In the 19th century phrenology was all the rage because it seemed to work, but we now know that phrenology is totally invalid. By relying on experience, thousands of phrenologists and their clients had been led astray. The same is happening in astrology.

We can now see the huge difference between the procedures of science and astrology. Science is evidence-based, astrology is experience-based. Science relies on nature, astrology relies on analogy and mythology (e.g., Mars the red planet indicates blood, anger and war). Science thrives on criticism, astrology drums critics out of the corps. As a result, astrology has nothing to do with reliable ideas tested against nature, and everything to do with unreliable experience.

Astrology Is Not Based on Solid Research

Astrologers generally ignore this unreliability, which nevertheless is more than enough to explain astrological claims ([Geoffrey] Dean et al. 1999, [psychology professor Barry] Beyerstein 1999). That is, astrology delivers nothing that cannot be explained by non-astrological factors. This conclusion is confirmed by decades of research into astrology, which has found nothing commensurate with astrological claims (Dean et al. 1996, Dean et al. 2000).

To put it another way, if the scientific study of celestial-terrestrial correlations can be considered "astrology", then one expects more than the banal nonspecific claim that "celestial-terrestrial correlations exist." One expects astrologers to provide testable explanations along with fruitful approaches to research. But in astrology such suggestions are entirely absent (read any astrology book).

Indeed, astrology lacks even the resources to provide such approaches. Thus appeals to analogy and mythology have gotten nowhere in solving problems for astrologers (Kelly 1997). A few astrologers recognise this, for example [astrology software designer Mark] McDonough (2000:1) points out that the confusion of chart factors now on offer is "because there has been no way to toss anything out."

As a result, astrology has been reduced to a mixture of factions, each of which supports its own claims with testimonials and self-serving non-threatening "studies" instead of stringent research. In any case, how would stringent research actually be used? Astrologers do not tell us how a factual discovery would explain the disagreement between astrologers on mostly everything (e.g. on which zodiac, house system, planets, aspects, to use), or how it would be incorporated into astrological practice with clients. Indeed, astrologers rarely incorporate *astrological* research findings into their work, let alone *celestial-terrestrial* research findings.

In short, in terms of procedure, "what astrologers do" is about as different from "what celestial-terrestrial scientists do" as one can get. Vaughan's argument to the contrary may have been relevant to what some astrologers were doing in the Middle Ages but not today (see [physics professor J. Bruce] Brackenridge 1980 for a brief history of scientific astrology).

Astrology Has Contributed Little to Science

Astrology had once motivated astronomers such as [Johannes] Kepler, albeit not others, such as Galileo. But for the last three centuries its influence on academic disciplines has been entirely absent. Birth charts did not help in discovering Uranus, Neptune, Pluto, asteroids, quasars, and black holes; or circadian rhythms, solar flares, geomagnetic disturbances, biological clocks, human geomagnetic effects, and bird navigation; or fractal geometry, the Gaia hypothesis, morphic resonance, and grand unification theories, despite the claim that all of these are astrology. Nor could they when astrology lacks the component essential to such discoveries, namely the critical testing and improvement of ideas.

In short, astrology since the 17th century has been spectacularly unfruitful in guiding our inquiries into nature. Which is why scientists and philosophers ignore astrology except for historical purposes, or for the insight it provides into the formation and maintenance of unwarranted beliefs. The reverse is also true. No astrology book cites celestial-terrestrial discoveries to support specific claims like Mars is aggressive, or that opposite sun signs are compatible (or not compatible). Nor do they consult Wolf numbers [regarding sunspots] or geomagnetic indices as part of a chart reading. And for a good reason—such areas are simply irrelevant to what astrologers actually do. In effect, in labelling parts of science as astrology, Vaughan is claiming that modern astrology is scientific, when in reality it could hardly be less scientific.

Finally, there are pragmatic reasons for rejecting Vaughan's claim. First, if astrology is so marvelous, if scientists are indeed dabbling in "what astrology has always known" (Vaughan 1996b:13), why aren't astrologers publishing in *Nature* and *Scientific American* and scooping the field? Vaughan (1998) says the answer is lack of staff, labs, and research grants. But who needs these things when horary astrology will supposedly answer any question? And there are plenty of even yes/no questions to be answered—is nature supersymmetric, is the cosmological constant really constant, does supergravity theory describe nature ([George] Johnson 2000)? If, as many astrologers claim, astrology is The Map to Reality, answering such questions should be child's play.

Second, if scientific research is so marvellous and so relevant to astrology, why does it play such a blatantly nonexistent role in the daily practice of astrologers? ...

Astrology Is Not a Scholarly Discipline

Astrology is completely unlike a scholarly discipline. In astrology, testimonials from astrologers and clients are the Gold Standard against which everything is evaluated; they over-rule the findings of studies, no matter how well conducted. If a study does not confirm what an astrology book says, then the study is in error, not the book. The dependence on testimomials is illustrated in *Astrology in the Year Zero* [by G. Phillipson], where astrologers say things along the following lines (the excerpts have been paraphrased):

> "Let me tell you about the amazing thing I did last week. The client had a daughter who suffered from headaches, so I looked at her birth chart and correctly identified the source of the headaches as a liver disease. And all without seeing either the mother or daughter." (p. 71).

"A man wanted to buy a ship. The horary chart had a Moon-Pluto conjunction in Scorpio on the IC, with the Moon applying, and I just *knew* that the bottom of that ship was rotten. Which it was." (p. 54)

"A woman lost her shawl. Her chart showed it was in a French restaurant a couple of doors away from her home." (p. 71)

"I looked at her birth chart and noted that Saturn and another planet were thirteen degrees from the cusp of the 4th house. I asked if she was raped by her father when she was 13, and she was." (p. 64)

"The astrology showed that it would rain all day, which it did." (p. 71)

In the astrological literature such stories are taken at face value. They are assumed to be meaningful and to provide powerful evidence for astrology. Interestingly, such a credulous attitude conflicts with the everyday experience of people in other areas. Thus we all know that stories and testimonials can be exaggerated, that they tend to improve with the telling, and that essential details can be left out. In science, stories and testimonials would merely be an incentive to conduct careful follow-up studies, but in astrology they are considered to be the end product, self-validating, error-free, and above criticism. . . .

Examples of "Research" Produced by Astrologers

McDonough (2000) notes that astrological theory offers little help in distinguishing between techniques that work much of the time, some of the time, or little of the time. So he suggests that astrologers need better qualitative research to set up hypotheses that can be examined on a larger scale by quantitative (statistical) studies. It sounds good, but we suspect that astrologers in general will not be interested, see . . . below.

As an example of the non-threatening "research" produced by astrologers, consider two articles published in the August/September issue of *The Mountain Astrologer*, which are typical of their type:

—In [astrometeorologist Ken] Paone's (2000) "Weather watches and warnings for August–September 2000", some of the predictions (which are mostly of storms) are testable while others could mean anything ("severe thunderstorms if moisture is available" p. 39). But there is no concern with actually following-up the claims, or with reconsidering what should happen if the claims were untrue. One might well ask, if astrology can predict a chaotic system like weather so well, why does the author not give a tally of hits and misses for his previous predictions? Why not challenge weather forecasters to beat astrology's accuracy? Evidently it is more comfortable for astrologers to have their heads in the clouds than their feet on the ground.

—In [Alexander] Markin's (2000) "The Astrology of Natural Disasters", the argument reduces to selecting a disaster and then finding something in the chart that fits, when the real question is whether the authentic chart fits better than some other chart. Without controls the exercise is pointless, so why bother?

Consider also the research of [Donna] Cunningham (1999) who went through an astrology data bank, extracted public figures sharing Venus-Neptune contacts, and looked for relevant themes in their biographies. Not surprisingly, nothing is uncovered that could possibly require a rethinking of basic premises. This is because looking for confirmation is always successful when one is dealing with symbolic associations; that is, we can *always* find some connection between any two symbols, as when astrologers accidentally fit a client to the wrong chart and nobody notices. Such studies cannot fail. Again, the real question is whether charts with Venus-Neptune contacts show more Venus-Neptune themes than charts without such contacts, but such questions are almost never considered by astrologers, including Cunningham. In any case the answers, if unwelcome, are without effect because astrologers always have ways to explain them away, for example the outcome was atypical or it was contradicted elsewhere in the chart. . . .

Astrology Relies on Untested Claims

Could astrology be scientific? Most certainly, since many astrological ideas could be tested against competing astrological ideas, against other symbolic perspectives such as numerology, and against competing ideas in the social sciences and biology. But this would require a change of epic proportions in astrological practice.

First, it would require that astrologers replace their dogmatic attitude that astrology is in some sense true by definition, with an open-minded attitude in which the truth of astrology has to be established by proper testing as in any other discipline. Second, it would require them to abandon appeals to analogies, testimonials, and unreliable experience. Third, because careful research has failed to find any astrological claim that cannot be explained by non-astrological factors, it would likely require much of astrological tradition to be abandoned.

The last is discussed by Dean et al. (2000), and is further illustrated by [Mark] Harrison (2000), who points out that traditional astrological connections with health persisted in British medical circles well into the 19th century, but were eventually abandoned when scientific viewpoints proved to be more fruitful.

Even if astrological effects were to be supported, their effect on people is likely to be trivial compared to other influences on people. Which is why [Christopher] Bagley (1999:32) says that at best "astrology can only offer partial explanations of human motivation and behavior", and [Suitbert] Ertel

(2000:70) says "I suspect [other] variables are too numerous to leave much room for additional astrological contributions."

Clearly, the logical consequence of adopting an evidence-based astrology instead of an experience-based astrology would be a huge restriction of astrological claims, and the elimination of much astrological practice with clients. Unsurprisingly, "most astrologers are completely unmoved by the results of all the research findings and statistics" (Geoffrey Cornelius 1998: 4). Or as Kelly (2000b) puts it, "Vested interests 1, scientific integrity 0."

References

1. Bagley C (1999). Identifying painters and politicians: A commentary on astrology as art and science. *Correlation* 18, 32–39.
2. Beyerstein B (1999). Social and Judgemental Biases That Make Inert Treatments Seem to Work. *Scientific Review of Alternative Medicine* 3(2), 17–35. http://hcrc.org/contrib/beyerst/inert.html
3. Brackenridge JB (1980). *A Short History of Scientific Astrology*. Dept of Physics and History. Lawrence University, Appleton, Wisc. Unpublished manuscript.
4. Cornelius G, Hyde M & Webster C (1995). *Astrology for Beginners*. Trumpington, Cambridge: Icon Books.
5. Cornelius G (1998). *Is Astrology Divination and Does It Matter?* Paper presented at the United Astrology Congress, May 22, Atlanta, Georgia.
6. Cunningham N (1999). Venus-Neptune Aspects: Dreams, Nightmares, and Visions of Love. *The Mountain Astrologer* 4, 12–18. Also available at http://www.astrobank.com/ASVenusNeptune.htm
7. Dean G & Mather A (1977). *Recent Advances in Natal Astrology: A Critical Review 1900–1976*. Subiaco, Western Australia: Analogic.
8. Dean G, Mather A, & Kelly IW (1996). Astrology. In Stein G (ed). *Encyclopedia of the Paranormal*. Buffalo, NY: Prometheus Books, 47–99.
9. Dean G, Mather A, & Kelly IW (1999). Astrology and Human Judgement. *Correlation* 17, 24–71. A comprehensive survey with 159 references. For a brief survey see previous reference, pages 89–94.
10. Dean G, Ertel S, Kelly IW, Mather A & Smit R (2000). Research into Astrology. In Phillipson G (ed). *Astrology in the Year Zero*. London: Flare Publications, 124–166. An expanded version with index will become available at http://www.smitpotze.demon.nl/Astrology-and-Science/index.htm
11. Dean G & Kelly IW (2001). Does astrology work? Astrology and skepticism 1975–2000. In Kurtz P (ed). *Skepticism: A 25-Year Retrospective*. Amherst NY: Prometheus Books.
12. Erlewine M (undated). Science and the lunation cycle. http://vzone.virgin.net/jason.davies4/Articles/lcycle.htm
13. Ertel S (2000). Reflections on Professor Bagley's Commentary. *Correlation* 18, 67–70.
14. Guinard P (1997). *Astral Matrix and Matricial Reason in Astrology*. Lecture given at the Kepler Day International Research Conference, London, 22 November.

15. Harrison M (2000). From medical astrology to medical astronomy: sol-lunar and planetary theories of disease in British medicine, c1700–1850. *British Journal for the History of Science* 33, 25–48.
16. Johnson G (2000). 10 Physics Questions to Ponder for a Millennium or Two. *The New York Times on the Web* 15 August. http://www.nytimes.com/library/national/Science/081500sci-physics-questions.html
17. Kelly IW (1997). Modern Astrology: A Critique. *Psychological Reports* 81, 1035–1066.
18. Kelly IW (1999). Debunking the Debunkers: A Response to an Astrologer's Debunking of Skeptics. *Skeptical Inquirer* 23, 37–43.
19. Kelly IW (2000a). Comments on Valerie Vaughan's "Re-bunking the debunkers." http://www.smitpotze.demon.nl/Astrology-and-Science/index.htm
20. Kelly IW (2000b). Vested interests 1, scientific integrity 0. *Skeptical Briefs* 10(1), 1–12, 15.
21. Landscheidt T (1994). *Astrologie: Hoffnung auf eine Wissenschaft?* [Astrology: Hope or Science?] Innsbruck: Resch.
22. McDonough M (2000). *Every astrologer a researcher.* Keynote address, Astro2000, Denver CO, 21 April. Available at http://www.astrodatabank.com/Astrology_Research.htm
23. Markin A (2000). The astrology of natural disasters. *The Mountain Astrologer* 92, 41–44.
24. Nègre A (1998). A transdisciplinary approach to science and astrology. cura.free.fr/quinq/02negre2.html
25. Paone K (2000). Weather watches and warnings for August–September 2000. *The Mountain Astrologer* 92, 35–40, 122.
26. Pennock RT (1999). *Tower of Babel: The Evidence Against the New Creationism.* Cambridge [MA]: Bradford/MIT Press.
27. Phillipson G (2000). *Astrology in the Year Zero.* London: Flare Publications. An excellent resource for both astrologers and critics. One of very few books to include the (mostly contradictory) views of astrologers, and the views of critics, on many topics.
28. Sober E (1999). *Testability.* Presidential Address to the Central Division of the American Philosophical Association. New Orleans, May.
29. Vaughan V (1995). The art of self-defence for astrologers: Lesson 1—fighting at the level of your opponent. *NCGR Memberletter* (Aug/Sept). Revised version at http://www.onereed.com/articles/revise.html
30. Vaughan V (1996a). Anti-astrology update: Debunking replaced by revisionism. *The Mountain Astrologer* (Jan). Revised version at http://www.onereed.com/articles/revise.html
31. Vaughan V (1996b). The acceptance of astrology in the Real World: Revival or revisionism? *The Mountain Astrologer* (Dec). Revised version at http://www.onereed.com/articles/revise.html
32. Vaughan V (1998). Debunking the debunkers: Lessons to be learned. *The Mountain Astrologer* (Aug/Sept). Complete version at http://www.onereed.com/articles/debunk.html
33. Vaughan V (1999a). A whole new way of looking at Libra. http://www.onereed.com/articles/vvlibra.html
34. Vaughan V (1999b). The celestial rhythm of sleep. http://www.strategicnewspapers.com/al/051500/alma.htm

35. Vaughan V (2000a). Re-bunking the debunkers. http://www.onereed.com/articles/rebunk.html

36. Vaughan V (2000b). Chronobiology: Astrology in a labcoat? StarIQ. httm://stariq.com/Main/Articles/P0000637.HTM

37. West JA (1991). *The Case for Astrology*. New York: Viking Press. Notable for deliberately ignoring unwelcome evidence.

Astrology Ignores Astronomical Realities

Phil Plait

In the following piece author Phil Plait argues that most astrologers tend to completely ignore even the simplest laws of astronomy. Plait explains that one piece of scientific knowledge astrologers ignore is known as astronomical precession, the gradual "drift" of constellations caused by the steady motion of Earth relative to the rest of the galaxy. Plait notes that over the course of the last two thousand years, this drift has moved all the zodiac signs roughly one full constellation west of their original positions, which means all Scorpios born in the last few centuries are actually Libras, Aquarians are actually Capricorns, and so on.

Plait also argues that astrologers conveniently ignore the mass and distance of objects in the universe when asserting their influence on us. He questions how, according to astrological predictions, objects as close to Earth as the moon and as distant as Jupiter can exercise the same level of influence on us.

Plait is an astronomer working in the astronomy and physics department at Sonoma State University. He is the author of Bad Astronomy: Misconceptions and Misuses Revealed, From Astrology to the Moon Landing "Hoax."

Let's get the conclusion of this article out of the way right now:

Astrology is a sham.

I've been saying astrology is a sham for years, as have a lot of other astronomers. We do this because the very basis of astrology is wrong. Many people I encounter wonder what all the fuss is about—after all, it's harmless dabbling, right? But

Phil Plait, "Bad Astronomy," *Night Sky*, May–June 2005, pp. 62–63. © 2005 New Track Media, LLC. All rights reserved. Reproduced by permission.

I'm not apologetic. It's hard enough to get people to appreciate the wonder and power of true science without mystical hooey clouding their thinking. People often believe in astrology because they think it's based on scientific principles. It's not.

While there are many different flavors of astrology, the basic premise of all of them is that, somehow, objects in the sky affect us here on Earth. There's some truth to that. The Sun certainly affects us, and we have tides from the Moon. And then there's the occasional asteroid or comet impact.

But astrology goes further. Typically, its practitioners claim that, through forces unknown, the arrangement of cosmic objects can determine human characteristics: personality types, predilections for making money, being good at sports, the ability to attract a mate. In almost every kind of astrology it's the planets that pull our puppet strings.

But how can this be? For a distant object to have an effect on us, it must apply some kind of force. However, the strength of every force known to science fades with distance. Take gravity, for example. Because Jupiter is so massive, it exerts a gravitational force thousands of times stronger than our Moon's. But because Jupiter is so much farther away, it hardly affects Earth at all. In fact, if we didn't have a Moon, the ocean tides raised by Jupiter would only be 0.0001 inch high—about the width of a human hair.

Many types of astrology, however, claim that the distance of a planet doesn't matter, and the planets' very different masses don't seem to matter either. The Moon, Mars, and Jupiter all exert the same influence on us. But if that's true, then an asteroid a hundred yards across should affect us as much as Jupiter does, and there are billions of objects at least that big in our solar system. So take your pick: either the influencing force fades with distance, or countless objects should be added to the astrological database. None of this seems to faze astrologers, and it certainly doesn't stop them from printing horoscopes.

House of the Writhing Sun

The astrological predictions you find in newspapers and magazines are probably the most popular form of astrology, and it's probably the most wrong as well.

It's usually called "Sun-sign" astrology because it's based on the position of the Sun in the sky relative to background stars. As Earth completes its orbit each year, the Sun's position slowly shifts with respect to the much more distant stars. This pathway around the sky, called the ecliptic, cuts through quite a few constellations. Ancient astrologers called these the "zodiac" constellations, and several thousand years ago they decreed that there were 12 of them: Pisces, Aries, Taurus, and so forth.

The idea back then was that whatever zodiacal "sign" was "ascendant" (rising on the horizon) at the exact moment of your birth would somehow influence your life. But that kind of precision was hard to come by, so latter-day astrologers settled for simply knowing where the Sun was along the ecliptic. In other words, if the Sun were in Taurus when you were born, then your personality would reflect characteristics of a bull. It's the basic tenet of Sun-sign astrology.

Well, folks, this idea is dead wrong.

Ask yourself: How can one-twelfth of the world's people have similar characteristics simply because they were all born at roughly the same time of year? Quite the contrary, many studies of personality traits have shown conclusively that there is no correlation with the time of one's birth, whether known precisely or not.

And for astrological purposes, exactly when does birth occur? When a baby's head pokes out of its mother? At the moment of conception? Does it matter whether the Sun is up or not? And if the alignments in the sky aren't favorable, should you delay birth to improve your child's prospects?

"What's Your Sign?"

Probably the most damning argument is that the constellations used by Sun-sign astrologers are incorrect. As explained in the [*Night Sky* magazine] March/April issue (page 56), Earth wobbles very slowly as it rotates, like a twirling top, causing our planet's spin axis to trace a big circle in the sky every 26,000 years or so. This precession means that the constellations shift with respect to our calendar by one zodiac sign every 2,200 years on average.

Astrologers' Sun signs were established so long ago that since then there's been substantial drift in the Sun's annual constellation trek. Were you born between September 23rd and October 22nd? If so, Sun-sign astrologers would say that you're a "Libra." But during those dates the Sun is in Virgo, not Libra!

Some astrologers just ignore the Sun's shift, relying instead on the constellations as originally created by their ancient predecessors. But precession is an ongoing process.

When was "Date Zero" on the astrological calendar?

Despite all the evidence that astrology is bunk, many people still believe in it. Even respected newspapers still publish Sun-sign astrology predictions. But maybe there's some hope. Even though I wish they didn't print them at all, I'm amused by where most newspapers print daily horoscopes: in the funny pages!

Whom to Believe?

There's a lot more to astrology than newspaper-style Sun-sign predictions, and some astrologers complain that scientists ignore this. But that's not true. After analyzing dozens of independent studies of astrology, University of Saskatoon psychology professor Ivan Kelly has come to a firm conclusion: astrology doesn't work. You can read his seminal paper, "The Concepts of Modern Astrology: A Critique," at www

.rudolfhsmit.nl/a-conc2.htm, where he thoroughly shreds astrological claims. As Kelly notes, "The conceptual basis of astrology is about as unsound as it can get short of pure fantasy."

Epilogue: Analyzing the Evidence

In 1955 French statistician and psychologist Michel Gauquelin claimed he had discovered unusual correlations between the birth dates of famous athletes and the astrological position of the planet Mars, a phenomenon he termed the "Mars Effect."

Gauquelin's results seem to strongly indicate a significantly higher probability that sports champions are born when Mars occupies a certain position in the eastern night sky, specifically a region that astrologers refer to as the "fourth quadrant." Such celestial conditions have in fact accompanied the births of many famous athletes like baseball legend Babe Ruth, boxing champion Muhammad Ali, tennis star Venus Williams (although not her younger sister Serena), and golf pro Tiger Woods. The odds of this occurring randomly is hard to determine for sure but the results were considered dramatic enough to cause quite a stir in the world scientific community when they first appeared.

Gauquelin's conclusions were eventually replicated by a group of Belgian scientists called the Para Committee, who published their own findings with reluctance before pointing out that much of their data had been supplied by Gauquelin himself.

An equally skeptical Harvard statistics professor named Marvin Zelen then randomly picked 303 athletes from Gauquelin's group of 17,000 and tested them for the same Mars-in-key-sector factor. His results seem to invalidate Gauquelin's conclusions, but critics charged that Zelen himself had used too small and arbitrary a subsample for his study to be effective. Zelen had also admitted going into the process that he was openly hostile to astrology. In addition, Zelen billed his results as an indictment of the Mars Effect in general rather than as a small, singular test of the base rate expectancy, which exposed him to charges of the same bias he himself had leveled at Gauquelin.

Gauquelin and Zelen were both respected statisticians, yet both drew vastly different conclusions by analyzing the same data. So who is right? Either of them?

Even other scientists who have conducted studies of their own in the decades since passionately disagree on what Gauquelin's experiments actually proved. We may never know the truth for sure. We can, however, acquire insight to help shape our opinion on the topic by critically analyzing the evidence presented and by weighing the respective paradoxes and questions left unanswered by both camps.

The articles in this book examine various types of evidence and theories advanced in favor of the authors' viewpoints on whether astrology is fact or fiction. Some articles that sound equally reasonable directly contradict one another. It is up to the reader to determine which articles present a valid case for- or against-astrology. The key to accomplishing this is to read the articles critically.

This does not mean that the reader should criticize the article by saying negative things about it. It means analyzing and evaluating what the author says, skeptically but with an open mind. This epilogue demonstrates how to develop a critical reading technique and apply it to examining the articles in this book.

The Author

One important factor to consider in evaluating an article is its author. Does the author have any unique qualifications for writing about the topic? For instance, an article written by a degreed astronomer or statistician who has conducted decades of field work using highly technical equipment should be accorded more credibility than an article written by the leader of a cult based at Stonehenge. Considering the author's background can help you decide if the information in the article is valid.

Hypothetical Reasoning

Sometimes you may know nothing about the author of an article. However, you can still evaluate an article on its own merits by using *hypothetical reasoning*. This is a scientific way of determining whether the author has made a persuasive case for his or her claims. (Hypothetical reasoning should not be viewed as an infallible means of evaluating the truth of an author's claims, but it can help readers ascertain if the author has presented a reasonable case in support of these claims.)

To use hypothetical reasoning to analyze an article, follow these five steps:

1. State the author's claim (the hypothesis).
2. Gather the author's evidence supporting the claim.
3. Examine the author's evidence.
4. Consider alternative hypotheses or explanations.
5. Draw a conclusion about the author's claim.

One thing to keep in mind is that while critically reading one article will help you determine if the article's argument is valid, you will need to read many articles and books before you can be confident that you have enough evidence to decide if astrology is a real phenomenon.

In the following sections we will use hypothetical reasoning to critically examine some of the articles in this book. You can practice applying the method to other articles.

1. State the Author's Hypothesis

A hypothesis is a statement that can be tested to determine the likelihood of its truth. To evaluate an article critically, you can begin by stating a hypothesis—in this case, a statement of the author's claim. Some articles contain more than one claim, but the author usually focuses on one major argument. The articles in this book each make one or more claims about astrology. Each article's title suggests the main claim the article is concerned with.

The following table shows the major claim of all but two articles in this book, reduced to a simple hypothesis.

Author	Hypothesis
Jackie Slevin	
Michelle Jacobs	Chaos theory supports the validity of astrological predictions.
Percy Seymour	Science has repeatedly confirmed the effectiveness of astrology.
John Anthony West	Astrology is magic that works.
Michael White	Astrology is a pseudoscience.
Lynne Kelly	Horoscopes mean nothing.
Ivan W. Kelly and Geoffrey Dean	
Phil Plait	The laws of astronomy make astrology impossible.

It is important to remember when you write a hypothesis that it should be a statement that is clear, specific, and provable. Look at the hypothesis for the Lynne Kelly article in the table above: "Horoscopes mean nothing." The language may appear clear and specific, but the wording is not strictly accurate. Horoscopes possess meaning to the astrologers who create them, not to mention their clients who pay for its interpretation. A more specific hypothesis could be restated like this:

Lynne Kelly	Horoscopes have no objective meaning.

Some authors like Michael White make several claims in a single article. To examine the article critically, you will need to state a hypothesis for each major claim.

Two articles in the table above do not have hypotheses listed. Read the articles and write a clear, specific, and (if possible) provable statement of the authors' claims in each of these articles.

2. Gather the Author's Supporting Evidence

Once you have a hypothesis, you must gather the evidence the author uses to support that hypothesis. The evidence is everything the author uses to prove that his or her claim is true.

Sometimes a single sentence is a piece of evidence; on other occasions a string of several paragraphs constitutes a piece of evidence. Look at the second article in Chapter 1 to see what kind of evidence Michael White offers to back up his claim that there is no scientific validity to astrology:

1. White claims that 90 percent of people shown a random, fabricated set of horoscope statements believed that the statements applied directly to them.

2. Most modern scientists consider astrology impossible.

3. White claims that calculating astrological birth charts requires only a rudimentary grasp of geometry and trigonometry and is not nearly as complex as astrologers claim.

4. Horoscopes are widely open to subjective interpretation and can therefore never be proven inaccurate.

5. White notes that there are many competing elitist and popularized schools of astrology, the rules of which often conflict with each other.

6. Newton's law of universal gravitation says that the gravitational influence of distant planets on a human's birth is negligible compared to that exerted by any and all earthly objects.

7. Tidal, nuclear, and magnetic forces are even weaker over distance than gravitational ones.

8. The few alternative scientific theories attempting to account for astrology are vague and reliant on mysterious jargon like that used by astrologers.

9. Despite the frequent invocation of his name by astrologers, scientist Michel Gauquelin's decades of experiments never yielded a theory on how astrology could work.

10. All of the subsequent efforts to replicate Gauquelin's results, including follow-ups by Gauquelin himself, failed to do so.

11. Constellations appear as patterns only from the arbitrary perspective of earthly human eyes.

12. All natal charts prepared before 1781 were based on the erroneous assumption our solar system had only six planets.

13. Western astrologers routinely ignore the concept of astronomical "precession" of Earth's rotation in their calculations.

3. Examine the Author's Supporting Evidence

An author may use many types of evidence to support his or her claims. An important factor to consider when reading an author is bias. Bias refers to preconceived notions that might prevent an author from evaluating the evidence objectively. Michael White refers to astrology as an "irritating puzzle [for] rationalists" and claims to be appalled at parties when "those we believe to be otherwise rational, intelligent people" profess even uncertainty on the topic. To White, the evidence against astrology is so overwhelming, the reader senses that he feels embarrassed even having to debunk it.

It is also important to recognize different types of evidence and to evaluate whether they actually support the author's claims. Michael White's article relies on four main forms of evidence: expert testimony, statements of fact, statistical evidence, and generalizations.

Expert testimony (items 3, 6, and 10). White does not claim to have had his own horoscope read. Instead, he cites research done by accredited astronomers, drawing heavily from their reasoned conclusions to buttress his own arguments. This is an example of expert testimony. Many writers support their claims with testimony from an expert or a celebrity. Many television ads do this as well. You have likely seen GAP commercials that have popular entertainers singing while wearing GAP jeans, along with commercials for aspirin and other medicines being praised by alleged doctors and pharmacists.

Advertisers know that many people are influenced when a celebrity or expert says something is true.

Celebrity testimony usually does not have much value as evidence: If a celebrity wears a certain brand of jeans, does it mean the jeans are good quality? Hardly. It means the celebrity was paid to say the jeans are good.

Expert testimony can provide valuable evidence, however. White himself is an expert, having been a science editor and scientific consultant, so when he claims that calculating a natal chart involves minimal mathematical skill, we are inclined to believe him.

White also provides detailed illustrations of his own analysis and cites respected scientists like Isaac Newton and Michel Gauquelin by name. If these sources did not exist or did not support White's findings, skeptics would be quick to point out these inconsistencies. White mentions the consensus of astronomers and invokes principles they are all familiar with, such as "precession." It is important that the cited experts are experts on the topic under discussion, and the author must provide enough information to help the reader judge whether this person is qualified on the topic. Michel Gauquelin was an esteemed professor of statistics who conducted decades of experiments on astrology. As the man who laid the foundations for modern physics, Isaac Newton is a more reputable source on the theory of gravity than Anna Nicole Smith.

Statements of fact (items 6, 7, 9, 10, 11, 12, and 13). A statement of fact presents information that can be confirmed as true. For example, the statement "All natal charts prepared before 1781 were based on the erroneous assumption that our solar system has only six planets" (item 12) is a statement of fact. The author states it as a fact, and it is a statement that is provable by investigation. Beware of statements that look like facts but cannot be confirmed. Ideally, to significantly support an author's claims, the statements of fact that he or she uses should be verifiable. They should be facts that can be looked

4. Consider Alternative Hypotheses

Once you have examined the types of evidence the author has provided and considered how valuable the evidence is in supporting the author's claims, consider whether the author has presented other possible explanations. If the author considers only one explanation for the evidence, he or she may be presenting a biased view or may not have fully considered the issue.

The most obvious alternative explanation for White's argument is, of course, that astrology is genuine. White considers the concept of human affairs being shaped in any way by the constellations too outlandish to contemplate on any level. For astrology to be real, everything that White believes about how the universe operates would have to be reconsidered from the ground up. Personality traits would be determined by what time of the year a person was born. Events occur only because they were preordained by the positions of the stars, the height of the sun, and other celestial phenomena. It is your job to decide if any of these scenarios are likelier than what the author is proposing.

5. Draw Your Own Conclusion

Finally, after considering the evidence and alternative explanations, it is time to make a judgment, to decide whether the hypothesis makes sense. You could tally up the evidence that does and does not support the hypothesis and see how many pros and cons you have. But that is simplistic. You will have to give more weight to some evidence. For instance, most of the evidence in White's article consists of expert testimony and fact-based statistics, which should be awarded more credibility than generalizations. You have to decide whether the author's conclusion makes sense based on how well he presents his findings. What do you think—does White adequately support the claim that astrology is a pseudoscience?

Exploring Further

Let's examine another article using hypothetical reasoning. Read Jackie Slevin's article "Scientific Tests Prove Astrology's Validity." First, it is important to notice that Slevin comes to this subject with a strong bias for its validity. Slevin is co-director of education for the National Council for Geocosmic Research, an organization that describes one of its purposes as "promoting and encouraging the highest professional standard and ethical behavior among astrologers." Thus, as you read her article, decide whether the author puts aside her bias and treats the subject as objectively as possible.

Now let's review Slevin's article using the steps for hypothetical reasoning.

1. State the Author's Hypothesis. Scientific tests validate that astrology works.

2. Gather the Author's Supporting Evidence.

1. The author notes that respected astrophysicist Percy Seymour claims astrology is a genuine magnetic force borne Earthward on solar winds and felt by us in the womb.

2. The author writes that respected statistician Michel Gauquelin conducted a test that found a high percentage of 576 French doctors tended to share similar birthdays.

3. A follow-up test conducted by Gauquelin of 508 prospective physicians also yielded the same results.

4. The author notes Seymour's observation that Gauquelin's results are of considerable scientific merit because they deal in "measurable quantities like planetary positions and birth times, as opposed to personality traits" and "indicate quite clearly that a physical agency is involved."

5. Sunspot researcher John H. Nelson claims that sunspots behave in ways science cannot explain but "is confident this will be done someday."

6. Though skeptical of astrology, Nelson allowed two astrologers to give him retroactive horoscope readings and admitted their results were "embarrassingly accurate" to a degree "beyond [his] comprehension."

7. The author reports that a 1988 survey performed by the National Science Foundation found that 38 percent of the populace believed astrology to be "very scientific" or "sort of scientific" and "six percent confessed to changing their plans to fit their horoscope."

3. Examine the Author's Supporting Evidence. In this article Slevin relies heavily on statistical evidence and expert testimony. She also uses statements of opinion, statements of fact, and eyewitness testimony.

Eyewitness testimony (item 6). Eyewitness testimony is a type of anecdotal evidence, a story or personal account that may or may not be verifiable (this contrasts with hard evidence, which is usually physical evidence or something measurable). According to Slevin's article, John H. Nelson reported that he personally met two astrologers who read his horoscope with sufficient accuracy to make him question his own skepticism on the topic.

Although eyewitnesses can provide valuable testimony about an event, it is not possible to verify their reports. We have only Nelson's word for it that the reading was unusually accurate, and his perceptions are shaped by his memory of the incident. Eyewitnesses will always remember some details and forget others. In addition, the longer it is from the time of the actual incident to the time the witness writes a report or is interviewed, the more likely it is that his or her memory will have changed some of the details.

You may be familiar with the common eyewitness memory experiment in which a group of people is sitting in a classroom listening to a lecture or doing some other classroom activity. Suddenly a stranger bursts onto the scene. The stranger may "rob" one of the witnesses or do something else dramatic. Then the stranger leaves.

A few moments later, the instructor asks the students to tell what they witnessed. Invariably, different students remember different things. One remembers that the stranger was of average height and weight; another recalls that he was thin or heavy. One remembers that he had red hair; another remembers that a hood covered the stranger's head. One remembers that he was carrying a weapon; another remembers that his hands were empty. And so on. When something unexpected happens, especially when it happens quickly or evokes great emotion, the mind is not prepared to remember details. This is why independent corroborating witnesses—witnesses who remember the same thing and who have not discussed it with each other—can be so important in any kind of investigation.

Another factor to consider in evaluating an eyewitness article is the witness's reputation. Does the witness have a reputation for honesty? Publicity-seeking? Exaggeration? Flakiness?

Statements of fact (items 2, 3, and 7). Review the section about statements of fact in the section of this epilogue that discusses Jackie Slevin's article. Then look at items 2, 3, and 7 and decide whether they are good evidence for Slevin's hypothesis.

Expert testimony (items 1, 2, 3, 4, 5, and 6). Does an expert discussing his field of research carry more weight than statements made by a layman? Do the professionals Slevin cites seem especially qualified to speak about astrology?

Statistical evidence (items 2, 3, and 7). Look over the information about statistical evidence in White's article, then decide if the figures Slevin cites can be considered good supporting evidence for her hypothesis.

Statements of opinion (items 1, 4, 5, 6, and 7). A statement of opinion cannot be proven true or false—it is simply what someone believes. (Statements of opinion are often based on or contain factual statements that can be verified. For example, "I think you are angry" is a statement of opinion but it can be verified when your face turns red and you hit me in the nose.)

Whether we accept a statement of opinion as good supporting evidence depends on the nature of the opinion and what we think of the person giving it. For example, if our history teacher says, "Peace in the Middle East will not happen for a very long time," we may accept that as evidence because we respect that teacher's knowledge about world events. But if the same teacher tells us, "Fashion models will be wearing white socks with black trousers next year," we may be less inclined to take this opinion seriously unless he or she clearly keeps up with the latest fashion trends or our history teacher also happens to be a celebrity (see *celebrity testimony*). How much of Slevin's hypothesis that science confirms the veracity of astrology is made up of opinions expressed by a few scientists?

4. Consider Alternative Hypotheses. Does Slevin consider alternative hypotheses? Does she consider explanations for any of the evidence that she admits remains unexplained? Can you think of alternative hypotheses she should have considered? Maybe Nelson's sunspot-behavior and Gauquelin's physician-birth-date experiments are simply unrelated phenomena. Maybe more mundane forces are at work. Maybe astrological forces are genuine but flow in the opposite direction, and our birth dates affect where the stars are, rather than the reverse.

5. Draw Your Own Conclusion. You decide: Does Jackie Slevin make a good case that science has proven that astrology works? What evidence most influences your decision?

Other Kinds of Evidence

Authors commonly use other types of evidence to support their claims. One of these is *physical evidence*. Astrology is unlike most other areas of mysticism because it rarely involves physical evidence that can be studied, outside of the stars themselves. If an article describes physical evidence, it should tell how the evidence was collected and investigated. Generally, a qualified investigator (someone who knows how to collect evidence without contaminating it) will photograph the evidence in place and then take samples to be analyzed in a lab or, preferably, in two or more independent laboratories.

Depending on the type of evidence, a laboratory can analyze it for chemical makeup, cell damage or mutation, magnetism, radiation, and various other things. The aim would be to discover if there is anything unusual about the sample or if, for example, a chunk of stone taken from a column of Stonehenge originated on another planet.

In addition to the stars and horoscope charts themselves, another form of physical evidence in the case of astrology is human beings. Where only a handful of people claim to have seen Bigfoot or been abducted by aliens, we all have horoscope signs. As products of any astrological worldview, we are all in effect forms of living physical evidence. This universal inclusiveness is one of astrology's main appeals.

Another important type of evidence is the *logical fallacy*. *Logic* comes from the Greek word for "reason." Logical thinking means to reason things out. (Hypothetical reasoning is a form of logical thinking.) A logical fallacy results from a failure to reason logically: You think you are reasoning logically, but are not. For example, you might make an overgeneralization: You say, "I have never met an astrologer who predicted my future based on my horoscope, therefore they do not exist." This may appear to be logical, but it is not. There are a lot of things you have not experienced that are real. For instance, you have not experienced spaceflight, the bubonic plague, or death, yet all exist.

Another kind of logical fallacy is a false analogy, or wrongly comparing two things based on a common quality. Here is an example:

> Honey bees make honey. Honey bees have yellow stripes.
>
> Wasps also have yellow stripes, so wasps must make honey.

The fallacy is that honey making has something to do with yellow stripes. Here is another example of a logical fallacy:

> My dog seems to sense when I will be home from school.
>
> My neighbor's dog also senses when he will be home from school.
>
> Therefore, all dogs sense when their owners will be home from school.

The fallacy here is that your sample is too small. There are millions of dogs in the world, and you know only two of them. This is far too few to make such a broad generalization.

As you read, carefully examine the author's logical thinking.

Now You Do It!

Choose one article from this book that has not already been analyzed and use hypothetical reasoning to determine if the author's evidence supports the hypothesis. Here is a form you can use:

Name of article_____ Author_____

1. State the author's hypothesis.

2. List the evidence.

3. Examine the evidence. For each item you have listed under number 2, state what type of evidence it is (statement of fact, eyewitness testimony, etc.) and evaluate it. Does it

appear to be valid evidence? Does it appear to support the author's hypothesis?

4. Consider alternative hypotheses. What alternative hypotheses does the author consider? Does he or she consider them fairly? If the author rejects them, does the rejection seem reasonable? Are there other alternative explanations you believe should be considered? Explain.

5. Draw your own conclusion about the hypothesis. Does the author adequately support his or her claim? Do you believe the author's hypothesis stands up? Explain.

For Further Research

Books

John Ankerberg and John Weldon, *Astrology: Do the Heavens Rule Our Destiny?* Eugene, OR: Harvest House, 1989.

Claude Benski et al., *The Mars Effect: A French Test of Over 1000 Sports Champions*. Amherst, NY: Prometheus, 1996.

John T. Burns, *Cosmic Influences on Humans, Animals and Plants: An Annotated Bibliography*. Lanham, MD: Scarecrow, 1997.

Roger B. Culver and Phillip A. Ianna, *Astrology: True or False? A Scientific Evaluation*. Buffalo, NY: Prometheus, 1988.

Geoffrey Dean, Arthur Mather, and Ivan W. Kelly, *Encyclopedia of the Paranormal*. Amherst, NY: Prometheus, 1996.

Malcolm Dean, *The Astrology Game*. New York: Beaufort, 1980.

Michel Gauquelin, *Neo-Astrology: A Copernican Revolution*. London: Arkana, 1991.

———, *The Truth About Astrology*. London: Basil Blackwell, 1983.

———, *Written in the Stars*. New York: Aquarian, 1988.

Steven Goldberg, *When Wish Replaces Thought: Why So Much of What You Believe Is False*. Buffalo, NY: Prometheus, 1991.

James H. Holden, *A History of Horoscopic Astrology: From the Babylonian Period to the Modern Age*. Tempe, AZ: American Federation of Astrologers, 1996.

Lawrence E. Jerome, *Astrology Disproved*. Amherst, NY: Prometheus, 1977.

Thomas Hardy Leahey and Grace Evans Leahey, *Psychology's Occult Doubles: Psychology and the Problem of Pseudoscience*. Chicago: Nelson-Hall, 1983.

Ronny Martens and Tim Trachet, *Making Sense of Astrology*. Amherst, NY: Prometheus, 1998.

Robert Parry, *Astrology's Complete Book of Self-Defence*. W. Foulsham, Slough, UK: Quantum, 1990.

James Randi, *The Mask of Nostradamus*. Buffalo, NY: Prometheus, 1993.

Gunter Sachs, *The Astrology File: Scientific Proof of the Link Between Star Signs and Human Behavior*. London: Orion, 1998.

Percy Seymour, *The Scientific Proof of Astrology: A Scientific Investigation of How the Stars Influence Human Life*. W. Foulsham, Slough, UK: Quantum, 1997.

Charles Strohmer, *America's Fascination with Astrology: Is It Healthy?* Greenville, SC: Emerald House, 1998.

John Anthony West, *The Case for Astrology*. New York: Viking, 1991.

Periodicals

J. Ashmum, "Astrology on the Internet: Quality of Discussion," *Correlation*, vol. 15, 1996.

Bart J. Bok and Margaret Walton Mayall, "Scientists Look at Astrology," *Scientific Monthly*, vol. 52, 1941.

Nick Campion, "Richard Dawkin's Attack on Astrology," *Astrological Journal*, vol. 38, 1996.

Amanda Cochrane, "Science, Art or Superstition?" *FOCUS*, November 1993.

Ray Crowe, "Astrology and the Scientific Method," *Psychological Reports*, vol. 67, 1990.

Geoffrey Dean, "Does Astrology Need to Be True? Part 2: The Answer Is No," *Skeptical Inquirer*, vol. 11, no. 3, 1987.

————, "The Truth of Astrology: Competition Entries Illustrate Faulty Reasoning," *Correlation*, vol. 16, no. 2, 1997.

Graham Douglas, "Why Is Venus Green? A Morphological Approach to Astrology," *Correlation*, vol. 18, no. 1, 1999.

Suitbert Ertel, "Raising the Hurdle for the Athletes' Mars Effect: Association Co-Varies with Eminence," *Journal of Scientific Exploration*, vol. 2, no. 1, 1988.

Andrew Fraknoi, "Your Astrology Defense Kit," *Sky and Telescope*, August 1989.

Michel Gauquelin, "Profession and Heredity Experiments: Computer Re-Analysis and New Investigations on the Same Material," *Correlation*, vol. 4, 1984.

Anthony Grafton, "Girolamo Cardano and the Tradition of Classical Astrology," *Proceedings of the American Philosophical Society*, vol. 142, no. 3, 1998.

Burton S. Guttman, "How Do You Solve a Problem Like a (Fritjof) Capra?" *Skeptical Inquirer*, vol. 29, no. 4, 2005.

Wout Heukelom, "Astrology Under Scrutiny," *Astrologie in Onderzoek*, vol. 13, November 2000.

Prudence Jones, "Foundations of Astrology," *Astrological Journal*, vol. 38, no. 5, 1996.

Ivan W. Kelly, "Modern Astrology: A Critique," *Psychological Reports*, vol. 82, 1998.

Michael Lindeman, "Motivation, Cognition and Pseudoscience," *Scandinavian Journal of Psychology*, vol. 39, 1998.

Kenneth Miller, "Star Struck: A Journey to the New Frontiers of the Zodiac," *Life*, July 1997.

Scott Montgomery, "Naming the Heavens: A Brief History of Earthly Projections," *Science as Culture*, vol. 5, 1996.

Jan Willem Nienhuys, "The Mars Effect in Retrospective," *Skeptical Inquirer*, November/December 1997.

Glenn Perry, "The New Paradigm and Post-modern Astrology," *Astrological Journal*, vol. 34, no. 3, 1991.

Percy Seymour, "The Case for the Defense," *Astronomy Now*, no. 11, 1996.

Victor Stenger, "New Age Physics: Has Science Found the Path to the Ultimate?" *Free Inquiry*, no. 16, 1996.

Richard Taylor, "The Meaning of Life," *Philosophy Now*, no. 24, 1999.

Jan Van Rooij, "Self-Concept in Terms of Astrological Sun Sign Traits," *Psychological Reports*, vol. 84, 1999.

Laurie Whitt, "Indices of Theory Promise," *Philosophy of Science*, no. 59, 1992.

Web Sites

The Scientific Exploration of Astrology (www.astrology-and-science.com). This Web site offers numerous articles on scientific research into astrology and debates over astrology's merits. The site purports that "the authors are mostly researchers who, unlike astrologers, have no vested interest in the outcome" and that "[a]rticles are rigorous, impartial, and have passed peer review," although some pieces also feature rebuttals and follow-ups by astrologers.

The *Mountain Astrologer* Magazine (www.mountainastrologer.com). The *Mountain Astrologer* offers myriad articles on a wide range of astrological topics, as well as astrology book reviews, compilations of statistical data, "astro-humor," and a daily calendar "outlining each day's aspects and the global astrological climate."

Horoscopes and Astrology by Astrodienst (www.astro.com). This Web site offers a variety of specialized horoscope calculation software in addition to articles by astrologers, seminars, directories on how to interpret charts, global news updates, as well as a bibliography and links to other relevant sites.

Index